SY 0090394 9

ST. MARY'S COLLEGE LIBRARY
BT12 6FE

SHELVED AT

920

KEL

Hens' Teeth and Other Rarities

ST. MARY'S COLLEGE   TRENCH HOUSE

This book is issued in accordance with current College
Library Regulations.

DATE DUE AT LIBRARY LAST STAMPED BELOW

-3. MAR. 1994

D1514303

Hens' Teeth and Other Rarities

by

Owen Kelly

GREYSTONE BOOKS
1990

First published by Greystone Books Ltd, 1990.

© Owen Kelly, 1990

All rights reserved. No part of this publication may be reproduced or transmitted in any form without the prior permission of the publisher and author.

ISBN 1 870157 10 9

ST. MARY'S COLLEGE
TRENCH HOUSE
BELFAST BT11 9GA

Drawings by Leslie Stannage.
Printed by W. & G. Baird Ltd at the Greystone Press, Antrim.

Contents

1 *Early Days*

The main disadvantage of being born at an early age is that you have to depend on hearsay for your earliest recollections. It is, or was at any rate, alleged of me that the first word I uttered was 'potatoes'. This may be true. On the other hand it may have been said to discredit me. That is rather unlikely. I had nothing worth being discredited for and by all accounts my contrary infant disposition was disrepute enough.

I was born in Drumderg, which is a quiet rural backwater of a place to this day. It's a stretch of half-decent farming country close to the foothills of the Sperrins, not level enough to be lowland, not hilly enough to be classified as mountain.

My father spent half the year farming and the other half in his flax mill. It was a small, water-powered establishment, fed by the water from a man-made dam, and working at full stretch it would never have needed more than five men to operate. Since at least one of these was the farmer whose flax was being scutched, and another was my father, it was hardly a centre of high employment.

I mention this only to clear up potential misunderstandings. Mentions of mills provoke quotations about dark Satanic structures, wisecracks about trouble at t' mill and hints that there must have been money in the family background. There was trouble of one form or another at the mill from time to time, but the other concepts are misconceived.

It just so happened that the slack time in farming coincided with the busy time in the flax business, which meant that the mill was a profitable sideline, nothing more, and my father was a workaholic, though the word hadn't been invented then.

Then was 1937, and a wee man with a moustache over in Berlin was building armies and concentration camps and making promises and enemies on a colossal scale. Less than 20 years before my father had come back from the other war to claim his inheritance. It wasn't a lot. Just a broken-down mill and a rundown farm.

He restored both to a measure of prosperity, which took him most of the next 18 years. As I grew up I formed the impression that he had enjoyed his war. The struggle against the Hun – his part in it anyway – involved a great deal of brawling with corporals and trying to put one over on a mysterious and awe-

1

some creature called a sergeant-major. I found it hard to decide which side who was on.

His last brush with military authority came on the day of his discharge, some minutes after he had officially ceased to be a member of the armed forces. The last gift of a grateful nation to its conscript gunner was, and my memory is clear on this, a mug of tea and a bun. He was about to eat this snack when he observed a German prisoner-of-war foraging for crumbs in the orderly room coal bucket, and on impulse he handed him the bun.

A corporal still in the service disapproved loudly and obscenely of this charitable act towards the late enemy and attempted to repossess the bun. My father, reacting to stripes in typical fashion, punched the corporal in the mouth and thus created an immediate dilemma for the military police. A brawling civilian in the orderly room, even if he was still in uniform, wasn't covered by military regulations. They solved the problem neatly by ejecting him from the camp, with a stern and totally unnecessary injunction never to come back. Since he had been conscripted in Glasgow and had no personal interest in the war, the warning was superfluous.

So he came home to the tranquillity of South Derry, to a farmhouse with mortgages rather than roses round the door. What with these complications and the agricultural slump that followed the end of hostilities, it was 1933 before he felt secure enough to take a wife.

That year he married Rose, the daughter of a neighbouring farmer, and over the next four years came Rosemary, followed by Brendan, then Malachy and finally myself. In 1939 my mother died. I was 14 months old and remember nothing about her. My only impression of her comes from a photograph taken soon after she married my father. She was a very good-looking woman with a gentle, slightly whimsical smile that somehow belied her prim pose and my father's formal stance beside the photographer's studio chair.

Her death led to the temporary splitting up of the family. Rosemary and Brendan stayed with my father, Malachy took up residence with an uncle in the village, and I moved in with my Aunt Mary, her husband, two sons and a daughter, about half a mile away.

Rumour had it that I could talk the foot off a pot before my mother died. I can neither confirm nor deny this, but I think it most unlikely. It seems, however, that I clammed up for a period after moving to live with Aunt Mary. Again, this is hearsay. I remember nothing about it. If report is to be believed, when I finally broke the silence, it was to utter the word 'potatoes', simply because Aunt Mary was at that moment preparing the dinner.

There was nothing new about children being slow to speak in those days. In their paradoxical way parents wanted them to learn to talk, encouraged them even, but the ancient maxim about children being seen and not heard was frequently quoted, which was more than somewhat confusing for a child. There was a seven-year-old on a nearby farm, for example, who had never once uttered a word in spite of the best attempts to get him to speak.

His mother and father prayed. They made pilgrimages. They consulted wise people who, in the way of ancient folk healers, were themselves crippled with rheumatism and lived in inaccessible places. As a last desperate resort they tried conventional medical opinion, again without result.

Then one day the bull got out of its pen and bore down upon the lad's unsuspecting father as he bent over some farmyard task. His life was saved by a strange voice yelling, 'Look out, the bull!' He leapt sideways to safety, convinced that his guardian angel had manifested itself, and the bull careered harmlessly past and into a field where it turned its attention to a couple of heifers.

The dazed parent looked around but there was only himself and his silent seven-year-old son in the yard.

'Who said that?' he demanded.

'Me,' was the child's laconic reply.

'But you spoke,' said the Da in amazement. 'You spoke. Why did you never speak before?'

'Never had anything to say before,' said the lad, lapsing into silence.

His second bout of silence lasted only until the following Monday, when he uttered a single protest as his mother brought him down to enrol at the local school. Before his outburst of filial loyalty revealed his vocal chords were in good working order there hadn't been much point in sending him to school.

He remained mostly silent during his schooldays except for occasionally expressing the opinion that it was all a bit of a cod. In fact he expressed no other view on anything until he emigrated to Australia. When he came back on a holiday many years later, he was prosperous but as laconic as ever, and he was heard to remark that Australia was a bit of a cod too.

Loquacity among the young was not highly prized in rural Ulster in those times, and so it's possible that my first utterance marked some kind of a watershed. Unlike the other lad, it didn't lead to immediate enrolment in school. That was still some way in the future for me.

2   Off to School

School had been hanging over my head as a species of threat for some time. I wasn't smart enough to make too many enquiries about the nature of the place, or what kind of barbaric rituals took place there. My apparent lack of reaction must have been something of a disappointment to the numerous visitors to the Aunt's house who kept drawing the subject and its attendant horrors to my attention. In fact, some primitive instinct compelled me to keep quiet, look daft and hope the whole notion would die a natural death.

It didn't. By degrees I reconciled myself to the prospect, and a gloomy one it was. I asked no questions, of course, but I gradually worked out that there was a master and a mistress there, and teachers. I had no idea what all these people did, apart from being violent and hostile towards the pupils. The pupils were often referred to as scholars, especially by the older folk, who used the word simply as a translation from the Irish. So with teachers, masters, mistresses, pupils and scholars all milling around in my head, with no clear image attached to any of them, it was a very confused five-year-old who set out for the first day at Draperstown Public Elementary School.

Pat McEldowney brought me on the first day. There was no codology in those days about your mother or father escorting you to the door. Apart from the teachers, the only adults I remember seeing about the school the whole time I was there were the parish priest, a regular visitor, the postman, who came often, and inspectors, who didn't come often but, even so, too often. Their visits had an infuriating effect on the teachers, who in turn worked it off on us.

Pat was a couple of years older than me and a very clever lad. Our way to school led past the oratory, a tiny chapel at the edge of the village. Pat decreed that we should step in and pray awhile. In view of what transpired down the years, I often wished afterwards that I had stayed a bit longer and prayed a bit harder.

As it was I just gawked around, for I had never been in this particular place of worship before, and like 'school', the word 'oratory' conveyed no clear concept at all to me. It was much smaller than the chapel we went to each Sunday, and I couldn't see the point of it. Of course, I kept this heretical notion to myself.

The parish of Ballinascreen, of which Draperstown is in a sense the capital, was no place in which to have deviant notions in the year of our Lord, 1942.

There were two women wearing headscarves in the oratory. One was praying and the other was arranging flowers.

'Is that Mrs Collins?' I asked Pat, in a thunderous whisper.

Father Collins was one of the curates, an imposing man of whom the parish was much more in awe than of the real boss. The parish priest was Father McGlinchey, a gentle and saintly old man and, as I was to learn much later, the flower arranger was his housekeeper, Miss McFadden. It never crossed my five-year-old mind that priests didn't have wives. However, even then I had absorbed enough about the local lay-clerical relationship to feel sure that any female inside the altar rails had to be Mrs Collins. Not Mrs McGlinchey.

Pat found my question hilarious. Miss McFadden got on with her flower arranging and ignored his wild whoop of glee. The second, prayerful one, reacted differently. She was out of her seat and down on us like the wrath of God before I had a chance to ask what the joke was. Pat's grin froze as she swept us out into the porch with a circling gesture of her right hand. He stepped smartly after her. I made a more leisurely exit. I needed time to fix my imbecilic grin in place. I always used it as a defence against unpleasantness and I had a notion that trouble awaited us in the porch.

'Who are you?' she demanded of me.

'He's starting today,' Pat said. He had taken on the job of spokesman.

Looking back on it now, I can see that she didn't want to make a scene in the porch and discourage a new client. She swooped into the pocket of her cardigan and came out with a threepenny bit which she placed in my hand, accompanied by the statement that I was a good boy. This error of judgement she never repeated during what was to be our long acquaintance. She was a teacher in the school and she went on her way without any reference to our unseemly display in the oratory.

I took a good look at the coin. Maybe there was something in this school business after all. Not that there was much you could do with a threepenny bit, for the war had three more years to run and the sweetie jars in the shops were empty relics of better times. Still, I thought, if you could rack up threepence a day just for going, the thing might have possibilities after all.

The illusion lasted only as far as the gate. That was where we met Danny Convery, a hardened veteran with a whole year of school behind him.

'Show him what you got,' Pat commanded. I flashed the threepenny bit in the palm of my hand.

'Who gave you that?' Danny asked. Threepenny bits were as rare as hens' teeth among five-year-olds in those days. Pat, still functioning as my voice, explained.

'Mind it,' said Danny. 'You'll never get another one.'

This kind of articulate cynicism might seem hard for modern adults to believe, but we were farm children and our vocabulary and attitudes were those of our elders. Linguistically, we went straight from babyhood to adulthood. Children who mastered the transition too efficiently were often described, unfairly, as old-fashioned.

It was the first day after the summer holidays and the village street was crowded with children making their reluctant way to the school down in Burnside. One gangly lad was eating a lemon, which is something I have never seen anyone do since. In fact I had never seen a lemon before and for all I knew it might have tasted like honey. It was obvious that he was showing off and he was surrounded by youngsters clamouring to know where he'd got it. Like a lot of other things, lemons hadn't been seen since before the war.

The war had much to do with the events of the next few minutes. Another lad, more cynical and old-fashioned than any of us, gave it as his opinion that the lemon had originated from the American camp on the Derrynoid Road. He further speculated that the forbidden fruit was part payment for services rendered by the owner's sister to any one of a number of soldiers stationed there. He specified the form these services might have taken, though my vocabulary wasn't sufficiently sophisticated to form much of a picture.

The lemon-eater made no reply to this, though he did punch the speaker in the mouth and walk on without even breaking his step. The injured party made a rapid recovery and, dripping blood, took a flying leap and landed on his assailant's back. The defender of his sister's honour walked on, with the offender on his back like a knapsack, until he caught up with a friend.

'Hold this,' he said and handed him the lemon. Then he shook his burden off and punched him several more times before finally throwing him contemptuously on the footpath, retrieving his lemon and walking on with his friend.

No morning journey to school was ever so dramatic after that.

3 Organised Bedlam

Education, at the lower end of the school at least, seemed to be carried out on the cattle drover principle. Tell them, tell them at the top of your voice and if that doesn't work, thump them. The school, however, only had four teachers to cope with the entire age range. This meant each teacher had two or three classes to cope with and there was a considerable amount of organised bedlam as well. The bedlam was due in part to the fact that there weren't enough seats to go around.

The village had outgrown its school by the time I became a pupil but there was neither money nor building space for expansion. Hemmed in on one side by the parochial house and by a stream on the other, with the street in front and a farmer's field at the back, the school could not be anything but over-crowded.

The result was that only written exercises were done sitting down. Reading, mental arithmetic, spelling and poetry were done standing round the sides of the classroom. While one or two of the classes in each room were engaged in these lessons, the rest were sitting down to their arithmetic, composition, geography or English lessons. This called for considerable organisational ability on the part of the staff, who had to teach two lessons simultaneously, and frequently at different levels.

The skills involved in keeping the operation running mattered nothing to many of the pupils, especially those more interested in the opportunities for skulduggery that the system made available. For example, the school had no corridor, and anyone coming out of the end classroom in the junior school had to pass through the infants' room, presided over by the eagle-eyed and very efficient Mrs McGurk. The two doors were in line with each other and at the side next to the street, so there was a passage left free along that side of the infants' classroom.

For the first couple of days I sat at the end of a row next to the passage, fascinated by the traffic going to the toilet. They went in twos, one walking, the other crawling on hands and knees. At first I thought it was all part of the system, but then I observed that while the walker was always different, only a small number of the same faces carried out the crawling part. One of the regulars was the lemon-sucking kid.

I discovered the truth before long. When one of the standing-up pupils in the end room asked for permission to go to the toilet, one of the sitting pupils near the door would, if the teacher's attention was diverted, drop silently to the floor and follow.

Travelling from the door of the end room to the outside door of the infants' room was hazardous to say the least. The crawler might find himself at Mrs McGurk's feet as she moved along the aisle interviewing the standing class on the subject of tables or spellings. Mostly, however, she conducted her inquisition from her desk at the front of the room at the side opposite the door.

The crawler had an even greater risk to face. There was a strip of open floor along the front of the room between her desk and the door and unless she was marking exercises, she was bound to spot him making his unauthorised exit. I never saw anyone caught in the act during my time in the infants' room, which is a tribute to the native cunning and gambling instincts of the crawler.

He had to cross no man's land in a flash and exit before the closing door did him a mischief. Timing was vital and many a time a crawler would have to take refuge under the desks as Mrs McGurk unexpectedly raised her head. This meant that he had to wait for the other pupil to come back from the toilet before he could get back into his own classroom.

The standing class would often enter into the spirit of the thing, and one or two of them would craftily drift away from the wall and block off the end of no man's land from Mrs McGurk's view. This was especially useful when the pair were coming back.

Apart from sheer bravado, the object of this exercise was the smoking of Woodbine butts which, like threepenny bits and hens' teeth, were thin on the ground in 1942. The ground, though, was where they came from.

When you consider the complicated nature of these curious exits and entrances, and the risk of being caught by not one but two teachers, both quick on the draw with the cane, it would seem much simpler just to ask to go to the toilet. That, however, would have been no fun at all.

Schooling during the war years was an unsophisticated business. A lot of stuff was learned by sheer repetition and tables, for example, played a large part in our early mathematical training. It was one of the standing-up lessons and we fervently chanted the lot in unison, from two ones are two, right up to 12 twelves being 144.

The table book contained a 13-times table but we were spared from having to learn that. Even so, that same table came in useful years later, when Draperstown school had passed into memory. I was going for an operation and I had read somewhere that people talk the most remarkable balderdash when recovering from a general anaesthetic. The article had recommended useful preventative measures, such as giving the subconscious something to work on just before going under. I had a go at the 13-times table. When I opened my eyes afterwards a nurse was smiling down at me and I asked her what I had been talking about as I came round.

'You were doing sums,' she said. 'And you were getting them all wrong.'

Mrs McGurk wouldn't have tolerated that for one moment. The memorising of tables, which included division, was checked by two methods. One was by reciting the whole thing from one to 12. There were many occasions, too painful to recall, when I fell, if not at the first hurdle then fairly soon after. The other, more insidious method, was used as a check. The teacher would pass from one victim to another, rapping out 'seven nines!' or 'four sevens!' and administer a stinging cuff on the ear to anyone who got it wrong, or even hesitated. You were also expected to know the tables backwards. It wasn't enough to know that four twelves made 48. If you couldn't grasp simultaneously that 12 fours also produced 48 you were in trouble.

The result of all this was that while the 13-times table may have let me down on the one and only time I ever tried to use it, I can recall every one of the others to this day. Mental arithmetic was a variation on the same theme, except that a touch of realism was sometimes injected, but this didn't add anything to our efficiency or accuracy. A query about the total cost of six calves at four pounds each might produce the answer, 24 pounds. On the other hand it might not. A farm boy, if goaded sufficiently by the irrelevance of it all, might dispute the price of a calf, and as far as pounds were concerned, the currency might as well have been coconuts. Nobody had any experience of either.

A great deal of importance was attached to reading aloud and this could be a confusing business. The books were written in standard English but the language in everyday use was anything but standard. Nobody bothered with the final 'g' of 'ing' and it would have tried the patience of nobler souls than our teachers to convince us about words like 'door' and 'poor'. Locally, a door was a dure, a floor was a flure but poor was simply poor. So if poor rhymes with dure, why couldn't a door be a dure and a floor be a flure? We were capable of rebellion over matters like that.

Since the teacher might be marking compositions at her desk – and interviewing their authors, sometimes painfully – she might be listening with only half-an-ear to us reading. We frequently followed our own inclinations in the matter of pronunciation. I remember one girl with a mutinous streak who decided that instead of reading out about a car being stuck fast in the mud, stook fast in the mood would serve just as well. This act of verbal vandalism was repeated by all of us with impunity, and passed unnoticed, since a number of perpetrators of grammatical crimes were facing the firing squad at the front of the room.

We all repeated the same words because a page of reading was set to be learned each night and we all read it. Those who couldn't read, or couldn't be bothered to learn, usually positioned themselves at the opposite end of the room from where the performance would begin. By the time their turn came they had it off by heart and could repeat it without even having the book in front of them.

The catechism posed the ultimate in memory feats. It was written without any concessions to young minds with limited vocabularies and taught without any explanation of its meaning. It began easily enough.

'Who created you and placed you in this world?' was the first question in lesson one.

'God' was the answer.

Before long you were into the heavy stuff, like 'Wherein consists the love we owe our neighbour?' That catechism was the only place I have ever seen the word 'wherein' written down. The answer ran to four lines of small print and ended with a tongue-twisting 'and in doing nothing unto others that we would not have done unto ourselves'.

We could all recite, with mechanical fervour, that we shouldn't do unto others what we would not have done unto ourselves. And immediately afterwards, either in the playground or on the way home, we did it. Without explanation, the lesson didn't take, you see.

Still, that wasn't the point. Once a year the Ecclesiastical Inspector descended on the school and quizzed everyone closely on the whole religious programme. Of course he got a full quota of word-perfect answers, learned at the point of the cane, but nobody understood a word of what they trotted out with such fake piety. I was much older when I learned that the performance of each class in each school was recorded in an annual report which was circulated to all parish priests.

Comments ranged from excellent down to fair. Anything less than excellent was unacceptable and the offending teacher could expect a dressing-down from the parish priest who was also the school manager and, therefore, the boss. The pressure was passed on down the line to those who were required to learn, as a reflex response, wherein consisted the love they owed their neighbour.

The parochial house was next door to the school and since Father Collins was in and out constantly on managerial matters, he would often pause on his way through to hold an on-the spot inquisition. He was an impressive figure, over six feet of ecclesiastical dignity, and his favourite query was about the content of

Sunday's sermon. There was a faint chance that if the question was posed to the right pupil early enough on Monday morning, he might get some small intelligent response. By midday it was very unlikely that anyone, except the most devout old ladies in the parish, would remember a word. Failure to answer would be followed by a meaningful look at the teacher. That in turn meant trouble in store.

My own case was complicated in another way. I was the only pupil in the school not attending the parish church, apart from the lucky handful of Protestant youngsters. They had the further advantage of a ten o'clock start each morning while the rest of us mangled the catechism. The sermon would be on the same topic in each of the parish's three churches but the treatment varied according to the preacher. On one-never-to-be-forgotten Monday morning the eye of Father Collins fell on me.

'What was the sermon about yesterday morning?' he demanded.

'There was no sermon, Father,' I said, smugly.

There were horrified gasps all round. He merely raised an eyebrow, shot his significant look at the teacher and went on his way. Such a thing was unheard of. No sermon on a Sunday. No dose of spiritual enlightenment for the natives in the outlying parts of the parish. Icicles formed on the ceiling. There was a deadly hush. Clearly, I was lying. She advanced on me like the wrath of God. The entire room waited to see me torn limb from limb. No sermon, indeed.

'What do you mean, there was no sermon?' she asked, deceptively calm.

'Father Doherty is away on his holidays,' I said

This sounds like a non-sequitur, but it wasn't. The church didn't close down for the fortnight. The holidaying curate had merely organised a vacationing academic clergyman to cover for him. Wisely, perhaps, Father Doherty seems to have advised him not to preach, a development the locals welcomed with barely concealed delight. I, too, shared in their joy.

Luckily for me, I wiped the smug look off my face just in time and some higher power replaced it with one of shining sincerity. Otherwise I might have got a foretaste of martyrdom that morning.

4 Cultural Affairs

When I was six months old, a generous relative bought a ballot ticket and put my name on it. The prize was a violin – a word no one in our district ever used. My name was duly drawn and I became the owner of the fiddle, for that was the preferred local word. Of course, I knew nothing of this at the time, or for years afterwards.

From time to time Aunt Mary, or some other member of the family, would produce the instrument and remind me that it was mine. I can remember some of these occasions, partly because of the expectant look that came over their faces as they dangled the fiddle in front of me. I had an uneasy feeling that I was supposed to react. With hindsight I realise they were looking for some portent that they had a musical prodigy on their hands.

I responded with my imbecilic look. The fiddle produced neither emotion nor curiosity in me. I would look from the polished fiddle to the bow and back again, wondering idly what all this had to do with me. Now of course, I can see that they thought my carefully nurtured bovine stare was actually a cultivated mask over seething emotions.

The seething emotions came later when I discovered that I was expected to learn to play the thing. Fiddle-playing was a useful social accomplishment in those days and boys learning the instrument attracted none of the derision endured by their urban brothers taking the more upmarket violin lessons. My fiddle was played regularly both by my cousin Brian and a neighbour, George Drennan, two young men whose machismo was beyond question. Most houses had a fiddle, and possibly an accordion or melodeon as well. A lot of men and women could produce music from them, and those who couldn't envied those who could.

Aunt Mary's conviction that the family's musical tradition was in good hands was reinforced on the day of that fateful ballot. I have often wondered since about that draw. Down the years I have come across a wide range of ballot prizes, not one of which I ever won, but my fiddle is the one and only instance of its kind. Naturally, I came to question the motives of the relative who invested that sixpence on my behalf. I have devoted a lot of thinking time to imagining the mental state of anyone who could even consider donating a fiddle as a prize in a draw.

It was the work, perhaps, of someone with a grudge against society. The donor may have been the parent of a child learning to play it. Driven beyond the limits of endurance by the results, possibly he had given it to the church bazaar on condition that his identity be kept a secret forever.

My views on the fiddle were out of step for my times and these thoughts, heretical as they are, I have kept to myself all these years. A neighbour called Jim Anderson confided to Aunt Mary that he was thinking of buying his son a good fiddle. He had detected signs of restlessness in the teenage lad and thought that a decent instrument would put any notions he might have about leaving home out of his head. Such was the esteem in which the fiddle was held.

I was present during this conversation and with every fibre of my being I was willing him to make Aunt Mary an offer. Telepathy failed. It was my fiddle, and regardless of any other views I might have on the matter, I was going to learn to play it. Her decision was pragmatic. Providence had sent me this instrument of aural torture. I would therefore make full use of it.

I was duly sent to Felix Mullin for lessons. Felix was the local saddler. There was no properly accredited fiddle teacher in the district but Felix was a traditional player of very considerable reputation. Like all enthusiasts he was a good teacher, with a sound understanding of both the theory and playing of the instrument. Still, even the best teacher in the world can't cope with a musical dyslexic and I never got much beyond the five lines, four spaces and the revelation that Every Good Boy Deserves Favours which marked the lines. I mastered the scales, in an excruciating sort of way, and could trudge through maybe half-a-dozen ceili dance tunes, but that was the sum total of a lengthy and, for Felix, frustrating course of tuition.

Felix was frequently engaged to play at barn dances and the house dances known as parties, and in a final effort to give me some sort of incentive he brought me along to several of these functions. It was a brave, even foolhardy thing to do. Fortunately, his being an accomplished player meant that his reputation wasn't even dented by the uninspired efforts of his disciple. He played music. In spite of the stimulus of public performance and the knowledge that derision would inevitably follow failure, I never produced any sounds distinguishable from a band of cats brawling over their love lives.

Playing at those dances wasn't an entire loss. Young though I was, I did pick up one or two ideas about the real purpose of dances. These were to stand me in good stead when I was old enough to go to dances on my own. Naturally I kept these ideas tucked away in the recesses of my mind since I realised that an innocent enquiry about what this or that couple might have been up to in the hayloft would certainly have brought about a rapid curtailment of my social life and education.

Dancing was, with one selective exemption in the case of the parish priest, a very desirable social accomplishment. Ceili dancing was particularly revered. It was known as Irish dancing. This was to distinguish it from all other forms of dancing, which were simply known as English dancing, and therefore decadent. Especially in the eyes of the purists, who took their cue from Father Collins.

A dance teacher was hired to teach the art and inner mystery of this cultural experience to hordes of youngsters in the parish hall every Saturday afternoon. Actually, it was the Gaelic hall but such was the intertwining of church and culture that one and all viewed it as the parish hall. It was a ramshackle building on the edge of the village with a flight of steps at the front and another flight up to the side door. It was home to the dramatics society, the organisers of concerts, whist drives, bazaars and above all, the Sunday night ceili.

That Sunday night ceili was a cultural must. I remember more than one ancient patriot sending their subscriptions by messenger when they were no longer able themselves to attend the ceili. A necessary apprenticeship to the Sunday night outing was served at the Saturday afternoon classes. There was a kind of unspoken lower age limit for the ceili. It varied from family to family but one thing was certain. Those who were painstakingly mastering the intricacies of the jigs and reels on Saturdays were far too young even to think about adult pursuits such as ceilis. Their target was the feis.

Draperstown Feis was the cultural event of the year. It was a colourful occasion for cut-throat competition and attracted entries from all over County Derry and beyond. There was much more to it than dancing of course. There was singing and verse-speaking. There was a craft competition attracting exhibits ranging from the exquisite to the hideous. There was adult team dancing and there was drama, and adjudicators from distant parts waxed eloquent on the finer points of each performance. The teachers looked smug or daggers, as the verdicts demanded.

I never missed the feis. It had one major attraction for me, it wasn't me prancing about on the back of a lorry-cum-stage, making a spectacle of myself. I also had the concealed, though widely shared, hope that some of the more exuberant performers would career off the back of the lorry and plummet into the crowd. None ever did.

My ever-optimistic aunt, only temporarily set back by my handlessness with the fiddle, thought I might fare better with my feet and enrolled me for the Saturday afternoon classes. I was sent, so I went. In those days a parental order was not a basis for discussion. I had no more enthusiasm for ceili dancing classes than I had had for the fiddle. This didn't prevent me from looking forward to the day when I could go to the ceilis and apply some of the secret wisdom I had garnered when, as Felix's disciple, I had been more interested in the activities in the haylofts than in playing 'The High Caul Cap' very badly.

My lack of enthusiasm soon communicated itself to Mr McCaffrey, the earnest young dancing teacher from Donegal. He despaired of my woodenness at an early stage and relegated me to the sidelines. The charade of the dancing classes continued for a decent period before Aunt Mary bowed to the superior wisdom of Mr McCaffrey and my Terpsichorean career was allowed to wilt. I was well pleased. It was no fun thundering unwillingly around the parish hall on a bright summer day when so many of my contemporaries were plundering the neighbours' apple trees, playing football or looking important on the back of their father's tractors.

Another source of gratification to me was that none of the craftwork displayed for mauling by adjudicators and public alike was the work of my own fair hands. As a general thing it was the prerogative of the girls of the county. There was a lot of needlework, embroidery and knitting, in the form of cushions and cushion covers. Occasionally a boy would enter a teapot stand or a blackthorn stick. The sticks would occasionally get a second or a third prize. The teapot stands didn't rate, and I thought that was a bit odd. I felt there was something not quite right about entering a blackthorn stick and getting a prize, however humble, for it. Nature did all the craftwork there, except for the lick of varnish, yet she never got a mention.

Still, it was a fine colourful day, partly because of the music and the dancing costumes with the Celtic designs, but mostly because of the opportunities to bump into relatives who could be counted on to delve into pockets or handbags and fish out a shilling or even a half-crown. This was an important dimension of the day's activities. The feis didn't simply attract culture vultures and folk on a day out. It drew like a magnet ice-cream vans, soft drink sellers, and a host of other peripatetic retailers.

Like the rest of the youngsters, at the end of the day I had to go home. For those old enough to go to them, there were three venues in the village for entertainment on a Sunday night. There was the inevitable victory ceili, which was just an ordinary ceili every other Sunday night. There was the dance in the Hibernian Hall. And there was the cinema. In the fullness of time I graduated to sampling all three, though not always with the blessing and approval of my elders and betters. Of course, what they didn't know didn't hurt them and it all did me a bit of good. I opted for the Hibernian Hall mostly. Hibernian means Irish, so the Hib Hall, as it was known, was the Irish Hall, just as the Gaelic Hall meant Irish Hall, but in that similarity lay a great contradiction. Irish though the Hib Hall might sound, it was the local home of English dancing. It mattered not a jot that a dance might orginate in Tibet, Paris or South America. It wasn't Irish, therefore it was English, especially to those like the parish priest, who was hot on Occasions of Sin. The hit parade of Occasions of Sin included the cinema, English Sunday papers, radio, drink, gambling, bad books, and any other factor that might pose a threat to the mythical purity of the Irish race. By the standards of ceili dancing, the Hib Hall was indeed a hands-on, decadent experience. After all, you put your right arm round the girl, you took her right hand in your left and you held her as close as she would allow as you shambled round the floor to the strains of St. Mary's Band from Park.

There was none of this licentiousness in the Gaelic Hall. Ceili dancing was energetic and demanding, but you didn't hold the girl. There were stages when you would swing her round or perhaps hold her hand but that was the lot. This could be more than somewhat frustrating when you watched a well-built girl jigging up and down opposite you while interesting parts of her moved independently of the music. It would have been a nice theological distinction to determine which form of dancing was sexually more interesting, and the question of holding a girl and experiencing whatever sensations that conveyed during one form of dance and observing her parade her wobbly bits in another, and working it all out in terms of eternal damnation would have been a suitable challenge for a Jesuit.

It would have been no sort of contest for anyone else. It all ended up the same way, which was seeing the girl home, or not, depending on the competition. What transpired in gateways and laneways was the logical outcome of what was transacted on the dance floor. And not wildly sinful, the way I remember it, when compared to the average everyday decadence of this more enlightened age.

On Sunday night, as on every other night of the week, the cinema was available to those who wanted nothing more demanding than to sit back and watch John Wayne winning World War Two single-handed. The cinema was suspect because it showed kissing. It also featured card-playing, which was sinful beyond words. Unless it was whist, twenty-fives or forty-fives and played in the Gaelic Hall for parochial fund-raising purposes. Card-playing on film was poker, which was unheard of, except in the back room of certain pubs, where pillars of the community would foregather after closing time for a relaxing couple of hands. One or two visiting clergy were known to take part in these games. Films were known to show people drinking whiskey, which was naturally a great affront to a community of 900 with 11 pubs to chose from.

The local cinema was in a builder's yard and for an outlay of ninepence you could sit on a hard bench and yell warnings to the hero as a fiendish Japanese soldier or treacherous Indian crept up behind him with knife in hand and murder in mind. For an extra shilling you could do exactly the same from a tip-up, upholstered seat.

There was a theory that in the comfort of the back row and with the right companion some of the more interesting action on the screen could be emulated. It was probably because of this notion that the cinema as a general concept, and our local establishment in particular, was defined as an Occasion of Sin. But no matter what the righteous or the self-righteous thought, no sin was ever committed in the back row of Draperstown's cinema. This wasn't for want of temptation, nor of willing young women – they weren't exactly an endangered species. It was because the audience had a sixth sense for rampant hormones. Visitors from more sophisticated areas soon found this out when, at the first hint of cafuffling in the back row, every head in the place swivelled through 180 degrees, every mouth whistled and every foot stamped. I never saw anybody who wanted to perform in front of, or indeed behind, a live audience.

For those who were of an age to act independently, rural social life, especially in winter, was an endless whirl in the late 40s and early 50s. In addition to Sunday night entertainment, and barn dances and house dances on Fridays, there was another Friday night activity that attracted widespread attention. It was known by the slightly misleading name of raffles. This may have been due to the moral ambivalence towards card-playing, for card-drives, which is what the raffles actually were, somehow didn't rate as gambling. There were organised knockout competitions, either twenty-fives or more usually forty-fives. Each farmhouse took it in turn to host the gathering and the winner got either a goose or a turkey. But since every farm had a flock of these birds for the Christmas trade, the competition was mostly an excuse for a night of banter and crack. Everybody was welcome. And everybody could play cards. Except me, that is.

If you couldn't sing, dance, or play an instrument or cards, your social prospects were bleak indeed. Everyone learned these skills, starting from their early schooldays. I had failed at the fiddle. I never could sing. As a dancer I was a menace. Aunt Mary and the relations pinned their hopes on the cards. I need hardly say that in spite of much patient coaching from my Uncle Barney, and my cousins Brian and Dan, I turned out to be hopeless at cards, too.

Oddly enough, I was the only one not concerned about my lack of acceptable community skills. My relatives may have despaired of my future but I never gave it a thought. I faced the 1950s without a care in the world. 1950 was the year I passed the qualifying examination, later dubbed the Eleven Plus, and headed off to grammar school. Perhaps if I had persevered with the dancing, stuck with the fiddle and mastered the cards, things might have taken an altogether different direction.

5   On the Altar

It was considered an honour to be chosen to be an altar boy, at least by female relatives of advanced years. The altar boys, for the most part, would have happily surrendered it.

Females, of course, were barred from the privilege and from the sanctuary except when, as members of the Altar Society, they cleaned, swept and polished the church from one end to the other. They were keen on the idea of young male relatives being altar boys because altar boys sometimes grew up to be priests.

One explanation sometimes advanced for the proliferation of priests in Ireland was that so many of their mothers wanted to be priests. In those days, as now, they were debarred by ecclesiastical contrariness from becoming priests. Unlike modern times, however, they were prepared to operate indirectly. A son, or a nephew, as an altar boy not only conferred kudos. It was not simply an outward sign of solid holiness, but a gesture towards what might yet be.

None of this cut much ice with the altar boys. I never met one who actually liked dressing up in surplice and soutane. To be fair there was an unspoken sympathy for the misfortunes of the dressed-up one. Lads who would otherwise have thought nothing of challenging others to 15 rounds, no holds barred, never poked fun at an altar boy for his poncey clothes. Of course it should be remembered that an altar boy was still a boy when all was said and done, and as capable as any other boy of blackening an eye or bloodying a nose the very minute he divested himself of his ceremonial garb. Or even before.

One day Father Collins invaded the classroom to announce that he was recruiting altar boys. There was a deafening silence. No boy moved a muscle, lest the priestly eye fall on him and sentence him to a lifetime of poncing about in a long black skirt and a short white blouse. Frilly, too. Father Collins pointed a random finger at half a dozen of us and ordered us to be in the parish church at noon on Saturday when he would begin the process of our ultimate sanctification by teaching us the necessary Latin.

This was fine for the other five. They lived in the village and the parish church was only about a mile away. I was affected by a geographical peculiarity. My Aunt Mary's house, where I lived, was much nearer to another church at Moneyneena. That's where all our family and relations went on Sunday. It was a rare occasion, a funeral or a wedding, that would have brought any of them as far afield as the parish church at Straw.

I didn't mention to anyone that I had been selected for the dressing up bit. Aunt Mary would have insisted that I should go for she was one of the old school who believed that the parish priest's word was law and no good would come to anyone who flouted it. I just excused myself from the training session, which just goes to show how naive I really was. There was no way, in those years, that you could thumb your nose, however figuratively or unintentionally, at a parish priest and not suffer his immediate and awful wrath.

Father Collins came into school on our heels on Monday morning and he pounced at once.

'Why weren't you at the practice on Saturday?' he demanded.

'It's not my chapel,' I said, which was just the way an adult might have said it. Except, of course, that no adult I knew would have had the temerity to say it. Right on cue, a look of horror crossed the teacher's face. A gut feeling told me that trouble was looming.

'Too far for you, is that it?' Father Collins enquired.

'Yes, Father,' I said.

'Hmm,' he said, and went on his way.

I didn't know then about the peculiar relationship between the teaching profession and the clergy. He had merely fingered me. The actual execution would be carried out by his hitwoman.

The door had scarcely clicked shut behind him when she descended on me like the avenging angel. The first right hook hurled me into the stack of rolled up maps at the back of the room.

'How dare you,' she yelled, waiting for me to get up. 'Of all the impertinence!' I rose to my feet and was instantly felled again.

The church militant was in excellent hands that morning. The smart thing to do would have been to remain prone, feigning unconsciousness or even death. Of course, I hadn't an ounce of wit. I got up and collected another right to the ear the moment I came within striking distance.

Apart from my injuries I was a raging mass of conflicting emotions that I could not express. I didn't want to dress up in the sissy gear. Even if they forced me into the ridiculous getup I wasn't going to be part of the altar boy establishment in the parish church. I had enough wit to realise that if I went along with this unjust imposition, it would cause serious disruption at home every Sunday morning. I would be going one way and everybody else another. The altar boy tail couldn't be expected to wag the majority dog.

All this should have been obvious to the teacher but that wasn't the point. I had defied the express will of the parish priest. I had rejected the honour of being an altar boy and turned my back on the pinnacles of holiness that might lead to.

Clearly, I was possessed by the devil, but the devil, as all old-style schoolteachers knew, could be thrashed out of his residence. It must have been the same devil who kept making me rise to face the fury of a female faced with one who had spurned what was denied to her, the opportunity to parade about the sanctuary in full view of the massed, praying public.

I wish I could say that justice and the rights of the individual triumphed. They didn't. Next Saturday at noon I was in the parish church along with the other five new recruits, learning things in Latin that I didn't even know in English. There was no translation.

My career as an altar boy was undistinguished. I completed my training in the parish church but never once served there. By some compromise I was attached to the team in Moneyneena church, which was logical enough but had a number of drawbacks. Not the least of these was the fact that the existing team all went to the local primary school and, of course, because of my temporary residence in my aunt's house I didn't. That made me an outsider in my own church.

The chief discomfort this brought was financial. Father O'Neill, the curate in those parts, would from time to time present two half-crowns to the leading altar boy, with instructions to divide them up between five. This made it a round shilling per boy. My arrival complicated the arithmetic and reduced the dividend. Given the prevailing mood I could easily have been cut out of the proceeds altogether. The deterrent factor was my older brother Malachy, whose brooding presence and willingness to take on all-comers ensured that no financial embarrassment ever arose.

There was a well defined pecking order in the altar boy business. When the full team turned out, and this was obligatory on Sundays, death being the only acceptable excuse for absence, we lined up three on each side of the altar steps. Only the two on the inside had a high profile. The lad on the inside right moved the Missal from one side of the altar to the other as required. Both he and the inside left fetched the wine and the water, draped the cloth over the altar rails and were generally very busy. The boy to the right of the inside right whacked the gong at the prescribed intervals. This was an influential job too, for each thud on the gong produced a knee-jerk response in the congregation.

This kind of power would occasionally go to the heads of those wielding it and I have vivid memories of a fierce struggle between

Malachy and Paddy Joe MeBride for possession of the tennis-ball-shaped item on a handle that kept the faithful doing their stuff. In the tussle they both lost their grip on the striker and it rolled away across the sanctuary, coming to rest against the altar rails and well out of reach. When the moment came to strike the gong Malachy produced a toy gun and whacked the gong with the butt of it as procedure required. It had the desired effect and nobody except the altar boys ever knew of the profane substitution. Apart from the actors centre stage the rest of the squad were simply extras who could have been dispensed with altogether, except that on occasion the roles were rotated.

The Latin, incomprehensible to begin with, wasn't improved by being delivered at breakneck speed in South Derry accents. It was, however, a rich source of hilarity for the more disrespectful uses it could be put to. *Dominus vobiscum* was often rendered as 'Dan, did the biscuits come' and *Et cum spiritu tuo* often came across as 'Ay, and the spirits too'. *Ad Deum qui Laetificat Juventutum Meam* was delivered from time to time as 'The dame shot a pussy cat and away ran a wean'. It was inevitable that *mea culpa, mea culpa, mea maxima culpa* should become 'Me a cowboy, me a cowboy, me a Mexican cowboy'.

None of this sacrilegious activity was known to the female relatives. God, look to their wit, was a popular local expression that still seems appropriate even after all these years. They sat in their seats, prayed fervently and in their minds' eyes they saw the altar boys evolve into the priests they would love to have become themselves.

My career as an altar boy ended during a parish mission when a brace of Redemptorists brought the sacerdotal strength at Moneyneena church temporarily up to three. Paddy Joe McBride and I were hanging about in the altar boys' room, sharing a Woodbine and waiting till our services should be required by one of the visiting priests.

Auntie Bea was an ancient lady who enjoyed the privilege during Mass of sitting on a chair by the door leading from the vestry into the sanctuary. The chair was placed on one side of a small passageway with five doors opening off it.

The attractions of the Woodbine palled. It occurred to us that we could while away the time more agreeably by walking past Auntie Bea, into the vestry, out through the window, into the passage by the outside door and doing it again. And again. Since she would see only two robed figures passing and not returning the same way, we hoped to create in the saintly lady's mind the illusion that there were hundreds, if not thousands of us. I don't suppose she noticed us at all but Father O'Neill did. He was coming round the side of the church when I landed at his feet, with Paddy Joe landing on top of me. He viewed our tangled and undignified persons, and excommunicated us at once from the sacred brotherhood of altar boys.

That was the end of it, as far as he was concerned, but not by any means for us. I recall the family inquest with total clarity. It's still to painful to talk about though.

6   Diversions

Michael, one of my cousins, arrived in school nearly half an hour late one morning. His hair was wet and there were angry weals on one side of his face.

'What kept you?' Master Gunn asked.

'I was drowning a hen,' said Michael, sullenly.

'And why,' the master asked, 'were you drowning a hen?'

We all wanted to know this. Surplus pups and kittens were drowned but there was no such thing in the rural economy as a surplus hen. Hens laid eggs as long as they could and then they ended up in the back of the poultry dealer's van or as Sunday's lunch.

'You told us that when somebody's drowning they hear music,' Michael said.

We swivelled our heads to the master. He had said something along these lines, though he was quoting from a poem at the time.

'You remember the oddest and least useful things,' he said. 'What has this to do with you being half an hour late?'

'Well,' said Michael crossly, 'I had my head nearly under the water beside the hen and I could hear nothing.'

Master Gunn surrendered to laughter and we all dutifully joined in. Then he asked 'What happened to the hen?'

'My mother caught me and took it off me,' the frustrated young scientist replied. The master eyed the weals on Michael's face.

'Come in,' he said, 'and take your place, you've had your share of hell.' He was quoting from another poem.

The laying hen was a power in the land when I was a youngster, so much so that it was even possible in those days to buy sunglasses for her. I no longer mention this in polite society. I gave it up because city folk were inclined to fall about laughing and refuse to believe that I had actually seen advertisements for hen's sunspecs on the back page of the *Farmer's Journal*. They weren't real sunglasses, of course, they were just spectacle-shaped pieces of black plastic used to blindfold the hen. This was to prevent her from pecking her own eggs, though whether they worked I don't know.

Hens were probably a lot smarter than anyone gave them credit for. Somewhere in their hearts they felt cheated. They laid an egg which they assumed would add to the next generation of hens. Instead, it ended up fried, boiled or in a cake. So they pecked their own eggs, not in search of calcium, but just to sabotage their owner's dastardly plan.

Delph eggs were another ploy. A hen would very often sneak away and lay her egg under some hedge, in an effort to keep her species going. The cunning farmer's wife would put a delph egg into her nest so that the hen would think, I've already laid an egg here, there's not much point in trying to hide any more, I'll just toe the line and do my duty.

In fact it would have been a remarkably dense hen who would have been fooled by a delph egg. It was smooth and cold, unlike the genuine article, which was warm and rough in texture. So the hens clucked their contempt and continued to lay out in the fields and under the hedges. This was a situation which I and my contemporaries could turn to advantage. A farmer's wife was always willing to pay a reward for information about the location of the extra-mural nests.

We discovered an unbelievable number of these hideaways in the laneways on the way home from school in summer. Unbeliev- able because we would occasionally fabricate the nests ourselves and place eggs in them that had come from perfectly respectable sources. On the occasions when we found real nests, we some- times split the treasure, placed parts of it in other nests we made ourselves and reported our findings to more than one farm. We were so smart I've often wondered since why we didn't end up rich.

I can remember hearing in a lesson on folk remedies that earache could be cured by applying a small bag of salt behind the affected ear. There was an epidemic of earache during my school- days due entirely to parental neglect. Our parents neglected to read the most up-to-date authors on child-rearing and clung instead to the notion that all forms of mutinous behaviour could be cured by a clip on the ear or on both ears.

There were several technical problems involved in this cure. How, for example, could we make a bag small enough to fit behind the ear? There was no point in asking the girls in the class for help with the needlework. There was practically no fraterni- sation between us and the girls. Since, as we were constantly being told, they were as good as gold, they had no first-hand experience of the agonies of earache. In any case, a direct hit on a bag of salt would probably have burst it. Also, parents had a predilection for looking behind the ears, especially after hasty encounters with soap and water.

The lesson on folk remedies also mentioned the widely held belief that the seventh son of a seventh son could cure a host of things, warts included. One lad was incautious enough to brag that he was the seventh son of a seventh son. We scoured the playground for warts but found not a single one. We brought him two boils, a sty and a nose-bleed but he was adamant. Find a wart or the show was off.

The next day a lad who had been off school for the previous three or four days turned up, complete with wart. We demanded a miracle and the gifted one informed us that he would effect the cure after school. We all foregathered in the entry opposite and he did try. He rubbed mud on the wart, he spat on it, he even prayed over it, but nothing happened.

The mob turned ugly. It was only a matter of time before they turned on the prophet and stoned him up the street. Master Gunn arrived in the nick of time. He informed us that the miracle-worker was the seventh child in his family, not the seventh son and that he had three sisters ahead of him on the baker's list. We had to find other diversions.

The watch was just coming into its own as a status symbol in those days. It didn't need to be accurate. It didn't even need to go. I do, however, remember the first time anyone in our class had a watch that really went. It was a nine days' wonder and we stood on the desks to see it. It was a chrome watch about the size of a jam-jar lid, with a shiny black strap and luminous hands. You could tell the time in the dark, the owner assured the audience, and we all thought that was a very useful thing indeed.

We were allowed to curl our fingers around it and see the green hands pulsing away in the artificial dark. Then the master came in and read us the riot act for standing on the furniture.

'What time is it anyway?' he asked, and the proud owner duly told him.

'What time would it be if you didn't have a watch?' the master enquired. None of us could answer that. Well, one lad eventually did come up with the answer and he wasn't supposed to be too bright. He emigrated to New York in later life and ended up owning most of the bits that the Mafia didn't control. So the local legend runs anyway.

The second watch to be acquired by a member of the class arrived from an uncle-cum-godfather working in London. A remarkable example of one-upmanship, it had a sweep second hand, a luminous dial, and it was shockproof. This, we were given to understand, was terribly important. The word 'shock' was then still in its infancy. A shock was something you got from electricity or from being caught in a neighbour's apple trees. We were anxious to know how a timepiece could be proof against either.

With the disdain that the new rich serve for the idle poor, the owner explained. Show us, we demanded, crowding around. The owner of the first watch stood by, observing closely. The

owner of the shockproof watch dropped it on the concrete square at the school door. The sweep hand stopped sweeping. A hush fell as he picked up the watch and held it to his ear. We had heard it rattling in transit from the ground to his ear and knew that no tick would ever emerge from its entrails again. With trembling hand he took a knife from his pocket – he was well supplied with the world's goods – and removed the back. Assorted springs and miniscule cog-wheels cascaded forth and hopped and trundled all over the concrete square and into the roadway.

It was an historic moment. If the watch had survived, it's possible that two factions would have emerged, each headed by a watch-owner. As it turned out, the first fellow left his watch at home after that and we all reverted to the ancient hierarchical structure based on skill at fighting, football and doing tricks on a bicycle.

During my schooldays I owned two bicycles. The first wasn't secondhand, more like twenty-second hand, as the purchase price of ten shillings might reveal. For all its venerable antiquity it survived a massive amount of abuse, until the day came when it could take no more and the back fork broke.

Worse news was to follow. It was made of some kind of metal that couldn't be welded, not even by the genius of Albert Page, the local all-round engineer, who could breathe new life into virtually every metal structure under the sun.

I effected a temporary repair by stuffing a piece of dowelling into the broken bits and taping over the joint with insulating tape. This worked fine for several minutes and then the other side of the fork broke in sympathy. It also developed a vengeful streak, for the broken bit caught in the wheel and catapulted me through a hedge with an eight foot drop on the other side. I got a cut or a bruise for very foot. The second bike cost all of 30 shillings and was a much more upmarket job, sufficiently so for it to be stolen almost at once. In South Derry lore, bicycle theft occupied much the same place as horse thievery did in the Wild West, and penalties were enforced on a do-it-yourself basis.

One of our neighbours had his bicycle stolen despite having taken the precaution – unusual at that time – of chaining it up. The word got out that the thief had left chain and padlock still intact when he made off with the bike. Our neighbour felt this was a slur on his honour and one day when he saw his bike outside a shop as he passed on the bus, he knew exactly what to do. He got off and stole it back. Any notion he might have entertained about his astuteness was dispelled as soon as he got home. The thief was waiting for him and a ritual exchange of abuse turned into a bout of fisticuffs which ended with our neighbour on the ground. The usurper then produced a spanner, removed the saddle and fished a piece of paper out of the frame with his name on it. Like all successful rustlers he had changed the brand.

I retrieved my 30-bob model in the same way, personally, and the rustler offered no resistance. The wheels were almost square. The temporary possessor had ridden it down the steps of the parochial hall for hours on end. Once I was allowed to bring it to school again, it spent the school hours in a yard across the street, behind a classmate's house. In exchange for letting him use it from time to time, he conferred on me a rare honour. He invited me to come home with him one day at lunch-time, to watch his father, whom he referred to as Our Joe, shaving in the kitchen.

Our Joe shaved in midweek and chose the most awkward spot in the house to do it. Between the door from the hall into the kitchen and the edge of the kitchen window there was a space about a foot wide. In this area hung a mirror, vital to the operation.

Our Joe brought a mug of hot water, a brush and shaving soap over to the window. Then he went and fetched a cut-throat razor and a strop. He attached the strop to the door frame and set about sharpening the razor. During this time and during the whole shaving operation, people came and went in a constant stream. Each time the door opened Joe edged to one side and continued with the stropping.

When the razor was sharpened to his satisfaction, he proceeded to lather his face. He stood in exactly the same spot, took the mirror from the wall, held it up in front of his face, shut his eyes tightly and soaped vigorously. And still the family came and went, ducking under his flailing right elbow. For the actual shaving he replaced the mirror on the wall, shut his eyes again and, still standing in front of it, he shaved away.

I was fascinated by the irrelevance of the mirror and the hazards of the busy junction.

'Does he never cut himself?' I asked.

'Never,' said his son proudly. 'Not even once.'

The school bell clanged across the street and we got up to go. Our Joe, his eyes still shut, moved out of the way to let us out. I wasn't as accomplished as the family at negotiating the door, the family dog, their cat and Our Joe. I stepped on the dog's tail and he followed me wrathfully to the front door and bit me on the back of the leg. Mine was the only blood spilled in this particular diversion.

7 Moving On

One of the advantages of being born in the late 1930s was that grammar school education was brought within the grasp of all for the first time. Of course, this didn't seem like much of an advantage to me when I reached the ripe old age of 11. Like the rest of my generation, my only ambition was to finish school and start work. I had no idea what sort of work I might be suited for. With hindsight I can see that I was suited for none. All I knew was that once you left school and went to work, you had reached man's estate.

By some mysterious process you acquired a bicycle and a pair of overalls, and the opportunity every morning to swagger a bit as the younger fry trudged off to school. You could circle them on your bike and jeer at them for having to spend the day cooped up in a classroom with Oul' So-And-So yelling at them. Then you went on your way to another day as an apprentice retailer, storeman or driver's helper, leaving them thinking how your life was full of fascinating things to do.

I remember the envy we felt at lunch-time when we saw the previous year's crop of leavers in their brown shop coats writing out dockets with a flourish and exchanging banter with the customers. We thought it was a great life altogether and we couldn't wait to be part of it. Especially when they lit up their cigarettes with a man-of-the-world gesture. The reality, that their lives were drudgery, and ill-paid drudgery at that, didn't strike us until many years later.

Few teenagers excited our envy quite as much as Frankie Halligan. He was known variously as Frankie Gawd Help Us, which is how his mother referred to him, except that she ran the words together so that he came out as Frankie Gawdelpus, and Misty Manners. He became Misty Manners because of a local farmer's inability to pronounce 'misdemeanours'. Frankie's name had been linked with misdemeanours from an early age.

The family were, as they say around Draperstown, decent people and the older Halligans were securely settled in useful and productive occupations. Frankie was, to use the local expression, a wee after-thought, and there was a long interval between the arrival of the second youngest Halligan and Frankie.

Frankie conferred no academic distinction on that decent woman, his mother. In fact he spent no more time in school than he could help. On the odd day when he did put in an appearance he usually left at lunch-time and spent the afternoon in the market yard, climbing over the cattle pens and talking to the farmers. They treated him as an equal, which they would never have done if he had been a farmer's son. His father was a house repairer who never used two words if one would do but preferred not to speak at all.

At the proper season Frankie would forsake the market yard and take up his position in Donnelly's apple trees. From this vantage point he diverted himself by pelting passers-by with crab apples. He developed a long-range delivery by impaling the fruit on the end of a sharpened stick and launching it after the style of a one-handed golf swing. This increased both range and velocity but not accuracy. The missiles fell at random so far from the launch site that for a long time nobody knew where they came from. An attempt by a local wag to spread a rumour that crab apples didn't grow at all but just fell from the sky at pre-ordained intervals somehow never got off the ground. He came to grief the day he felled a lady as she cycled sedately along the main road almost 100 yards away. He boasted of his exploit, which is an unwise thing to do in a village. Within hours his victim was parading her bruises at Halligan's front door, demanding retribution. It was this incident which earned him, from the target's husband, the nickname Misty Manners.

Mrs Halligan made another attempt to thrash the devil out of her erring son but Frankie's demon seemed to thrive on punishment. He left school unable to read or write and embarked on the career of laundry van driver's helper, but he wasn't much help to the driver. This was partly because he couldn't read the names and addresses on the parcels and partly because really he only wanted to drive the van. He had been driving vans from the age of eight, sometimes with, and just as often without, the owner's consent.

The crunch came one hot summer afternoon when the driver, fed up with having to drive his helper to the door of every call, got out to deliver a parcel himself. Almost absent-mindedly, Frankie slipped into the driving seat and drove off. By all accounts he had a fine time, racing up hill and down dale without benefit of licence or insurance. He brought the van back without a scratch and without petrol, having coasted the last few hundred yards downhill into the village. The casualty toll for the afternoon was one hen, one duck and Frankie's job.

The dead duck posed a problem. Hens are flighty and indecisive creatures and must take their chances when crossing the road. Ducks, on the other hand, are single-minded and therefore have right of way and enjoy the full protection of the law. The demise of the duck cost Mrs Halligan money, for which she extracted full value from Frankie's hide.

His father clung to the view that Frankie would turn out all right in the end. Clung, is perhaps the wrong word, since he expressed it only once in public hearing and that was when he met a teacher in the street. She had been goaded beyond endurance by Frankie's antics, and when Old Man Halligan, in one of his rare communicative moods, asked her for her opinion of his son, she told him crisply that Frankie was ineducable. The father thought this was some kind of dreadful disease and was deeply shaken. When she explained, he let out a great shout of laughter and informed everyone within earshot that Frankie would do all right in the end.

Then one day it emerged that Frankie had left home. The village was divided over the cause. A certain body of opinion held that Mrs Halligan had simply ordered him off the premises. The supporters of this view managed to create the impression that they had had a grandstand view of the expulsion. They quoted, in some detail, Mrs Halligan's strictures about her son's voracious appetite, the bad company he kept and his generally unproductive way of life.

The truth was Frankie had discovered beer. Not on a very grand scale but then he was inexperienced at this new activity and a little went a long way. There was no doubt in the collective mind that if Mrs Halligan should get to hear of this development there would be trouble for her youngest son on an unprecedented scale. Old Man Halligan's reaction would be uncertain but could be expected to be broadly disapproving.

It wasn't the sort of thing that even the most benevolent of conspiracies could keep hidden for long but Frankie was the author of his own misfortune. Local legend was precise on the details.

It seems that Old Man Halligan returned from his usual stroll late one night and tripped over Frankie's paralytic form on the garden path. It is said that he made an economical pronouncement to the effect that he had had enough of Frankie and his carry-on, and that one of them would have to go. Frankie is said to have raised himself on one elbow, focussed with some difficulty on his outraged parent and spoke. 'You'd better go, Da,' he said. 'I'm too drunk.'

This brief exchange ended with Frankie running for his life, pursued by his father, pelting him with his belongings.

That was the last the village ever saw of Frankie. He did, however, justify his father's prophecy that he would do all right in the end. Some years later Old Man Halligan tracked him down in the English Midlands and wasn't in the least surprised to find he was the owner of a chain of flourishing greengrocery shops.

His van driving skills had been the making of him. He had got a job driving a greengrocer's van because the owner had been disqualified on a drink-driving charge. He simply drove and the boss did all the buying and selling.

One day, however, the boss sent him to the market on his own to collect a bag of potatoes and deliver them to an hotel. He gave him three pounds to pay for the potatoes and the hotel manager gave him six pounds to bring back to the shop.

'That's when he decided to start up a business for himself,' Old Man Halligan said, many years later. 'Our Frankie was never much good at counting but he could count up to three twice. He told me he knew he'd be all right so long as he could make that three per cent on every deal.' The early adventures of Frankie and his contemporaries seemed glamorous to me but I never became part of that world.

One day Master Gunn had a brief conversation with someone out of sight below the level of the school's high windows, then he turned back and told me that I was going to do the qualifying exam. The someone out of sight was my father. That, of course, was how things were done in those days. He hadn't taken me into his confidence about either the exam or his visit to the school. Parents didn't feel the need to explain themselves. Far-reaching decisions were made without consultation and the results conveyed casually some time later.

Entry for the examination wasn't compulsory but in Drapers-town as everywhere else, the new, free secondary system beckoned urgently to parents looking for something better for their children. Virtually all the class were potential candidates. The process began with an intelligence test, then there was an arithmetic paper and an English test at a later stage.

The exam and its standards were very much an unknown quantity in those early days, so nothing was left to chance. The English and arithmetic syllabuses were comprehensive, and exhausting. As the pressures mounted, the number of hopefuls declined. I envied them. They had a fine time, drawing and reading, while Jim Gunn rehearsed us in the written papers. He was an extraordinarily patient man. He had been a promising athlete in his youth, and outdoor pursuits of all kinds appealed to him all his life. A dog and gun man, an angler, equally at home in the woods or on the mountain, his ruddy complexion and silvery hair, tweed jackets and flannels gave him the air of a traditional country squire.

A tremendously humorous man, he had several characteristics that made him popular with his pupils. He disapproved of homework, on sound educational grounds which he explained to us. There were those pupils, he said, who could do it with their eyes shut. They would learn nothing from it. Others would get it done for them, so they would be no better off. The rest wouldn't bother at all, with the same result. The time thus saved from marking homework and listening to excuses was made available for extra lessons in school. Another pleasant thing about the atmosphere in his classroom was his opposition to corporal punishment. His commanding personality and a peculiar frown he had perfected involving the use of one bushy eyebrow were his only disciplinary aids.

The first time I was ever in a taxi was when I went to do the exam. By that time the number of hopefuls had declined sufficiently for one car to transport us all to the Rainey Endowed School in Magherafelt, the examination centre for South Derry. The Rainey, as it was popularly known, was a Protestant school in reality, though not in theory. It was intended as a non-denominational school but in practice few Catholics attended it. This was partly due to Catholic church policy and partly to the relatively small numbers of Catholics going into second-level education in pre-Eleven Plus days.

The examination itself was a forgettable experience, but I remember the day well for another reason. It was the first time I have ever seen a school with a dining hall. Lunch-time in Draperstown school was a matter of munching the sandwich lunch in a corner of the playground. I had read about more civilised amenities in books and comics, but I was suitably overawed the first time I saw them for myself.

We had been well-warned beforehand to be on our best behaviour in the Rainey and not to let the side down in the eyes of the Protestant middle class. In fact the only untoward incident in the dining room was when a boy in Rainey uniform sought to attract the attention of various acquaintances in different areas of the dining room by hurling spoons at them. He bent the spoons first of all, which was the first piece of school vandalism I had ever seen. Nobody took the least notice of this behaviour, not even the master in the black gown who was patrolling the room.

When the results came out, in late May, nobody was more surprised than I was to discover that I'd passed. There was a useful bonus in this achievement. The tradition had already begun, though it was only the second year of the exam, that once you passed, your primary school education had come to an end. You simply didn't turn up for school any more. This meant the summer holidays were extended by about six weeks. Obviously there must have been some form of official blessing for this lengthy absenteeism.

I went home that afternoon and tossed my schoolbag into the barn. I was never going to need it again, or so I thought. In all the family euphoria about my examination success, one important detail had been overlooked. No one had staked a claim on a school place for me. The only school available was St Columb's College, a boarding establishment in Derry. It's true that Rainey Endowed was in Magherafelt, only eight miles away, and its doors were open to all qualified comers, but Catholics were discouraged by episcopal edict from attending it.

St Columb's, with a huge catchment area and limited accommodation for pupils living in, couldn't take all applicants. Shrewd folk, presumably, put their sons' names down long before the exam and withdrew them if the results were unfavourable. My father preferred to wait for the outcome, and in my case this was too late. Not even the fact that my brother Malachy was already a pupil at St Columb's cut any ice. The headmaster, officially known as the president, informed us that I would have to wait until the following year.

In September I had to retrieve my schoolbag from the barn and go back to primary school. Other indignities were to follow. Along with one other pupil, Donal McKee, I had passed the exam as an under-age candidate. His parents, like mine, had waited too long too for a place for him, so he was compelled to repeat the year, too. We formed an instant and unholy alliance. Although our places were secured for the following year, it was decreed at some higher level that we should do the exam again. There was no guarantee that we could repeat our performance. We were allowed to voice this doubt but symbolic protest was all we were permitted. We were told, in any case, that the previous year's result would stand. Our chief role was to be makeweights.

8   *The Legend of Genghis McCann*

Worse, much worse, was to befall. Jim Gunn was struck down by some mysterious illness which meant a long absence from school. His place was taken by a female thug, a species of abominable snowman in tweeds, with a simple educational philosophy: thrash them often enough and hard enough, and they'll learn anything.

This approach to education was the rule in those days. Jim Gunn's enlightened attitude was the exception and so her arrival was a severe shock. She was instantly dubbed the Fearful Fogarty One, though how this oddly appropriate nickname came about was never clear. By means of that curious freemasonry that exists among rebellious children she became the Fearful Fogarty One within the first hour of her first day. And so she remained until, in the fullness of time, Jim Gunn returned to prepare another bunch for a tussle with the qualifying examination.

Homework, unknown under Jim's benevolent regime, became the order of the day. No excuses were accepted. Even Paddy Conroy, who had genuinely sharpened his finger instead of his pencil with his brand-new penknife and had real blood dripping from it, was callously told to write with the other hand. There was no library period, no storytelling sessions, no art, just work and more work. Donal and I decided that we'd had enough. One morning after roll call, we dropped on all fours when her back was turned and slipped out in the time-honoured fashion through the infants' room.

We were marked present. The entire age range of the school was divided over three teachers, so the classes were big and we were unlikely to be missed. We marched up the village street as though we'd bought and paid for every stone of it, crossed the Fair Hill, skirted the wall of the Church of Ireland cemetery and marched along the river bank to where Donal had attached a length of rope to an overhanging branch.

War films were all the rage then, and all of us had completed our commando training in the village cinema, so we spent an agreeable hour swinging back and forth across the river, and liberating vast tracts of territory from Johnny O'Hagan's puzzled cows. Then Donal fell in the river. We went to his house. His

41

father was at work, his mother was at her mother's. So he just changed into dry clothes and we decided to sneak back into school.

'What will you tell your mother about the wet clothes?' I asked him, as we dawdled down the street.

'Nothing,' he replied, confidently. 'I left them on a chair under the window. Later on I'll pray for rain.'

I was puzzling over this extraordinary expression of faith when I saw the sixpence lying on the pavement. We went and invested it in a bar of chocolate. As we were dividing it by the pump at the school gate, a low-flying pigeon dive-bombed it with perfect accuracy, right in the middle. We were still looking at each other in stunned silence at this unlucky turn of events when the Fearful Fogarty emerged like a whirlwind from the school and addressed us in tones that brought work in Joe Leyden's forge across the street to a standstill.

'What are you two villains doing out here?' she asked, at the top of her considerable voice.

'We were at the toilet, Miss,' said Donal, in precisely the same confident tones he had used to assure me that the Almighty would send a shower of rain to cover up his mitching, 'and we were just washing our hands.'

She looked from him to me and back, taking in the many-hued, evil-smelling mass on the way. She swelled and shrank once or twice and then pointed silently at the door. We went in. And that, inexplicably, uncharacteristically, was the end of the matter. No execution followed. Perhaps she discerned in Donal some hint of the headmaster and pillar of the community he was to become in future years. His blessed aura must have saved me. She got me the next time round. This was the day a legend was born in our school. He was John Philip McCann, a lad completely unmoved by education.

His outstanding attributes were an extensive vocabulary of hair-raising invective and an unorthodox but effective skill in brawling. This talent ensured him a near-permanent spot in the limelight, in the form of bloody encounters with the youth of the village.

Basically Draperstown was cross-shaped, with four converging wide streets consisting of a random assortment of houses and shops. Even though its population was less than 1,000 and you could be in open country after two minutes' brisk walk in any direction from the middle, there was a certain amount of snobbery among some of the villagers about country people. The sons of the commercial houses had little time for farm boys, but any airs of urban sophistication they adopted were whittled down to size by McCann and his versatile vocabulary. The village lads were touchy about their status. They were reared on a diet of *The*

Wizard, *The Hotspur*, *Adventure* and the codes of honour and sportsmanship enshrined therein.

None of this cut any ice with McCann. His strategy, like all good strategies, was simple. When he got involved in fisticuffs, he lured his Queensberry Rules' opponent into a suitable corner – Conville's Corner by the bus-stop was his favourite – and there converted himself into a hob-nailed hedgehog. He wedged his right shoulder against the wall and his steel-shod left heel flashed with deadly effect up and down the shins, knees or other vulnerable areas of his opponent's frontage. It says a lot for the fortitude of the village champions that in spite of the certain knowledge that they would be defeated they still hurled themselves against the lethal heel. It was magnificent, of course, but it was no contest.

McCann's talent for aggravation wasn't limited to the village boys. His mere existence was an affront to the Fearful Fogarty One. He neither learned nor made any effort to learn and, hardened both by his brawling and long hours of toil on the farm, he took his punishment in his stride. Never once did he wince. This infuriated her, and so she reserved her particular venom for McCann and, because I was invariably involved in his exploits, for me, too. Our classmates, they of the scarred shins, sometimes expressed pseudo-sympathy, in attempts to make common cause in adversity. His invariable reply was, 'Ah, to hell with her.' Those are not his exact words. I have cleaned them up considerably.

McCann's conversion from cornerboy hoodlum to folk hero came about by accident. It seems that an inspection was due. The Fearful Fogarty One was determined to show the Man from the Ministry that she had talents other than cattle-droving. One Friday afternoon she produced a folder and put up a series of pictures around the walls. The purpose behind this display of erudition was twofold. It covered up a lot of damp spots and gave the place an air of culture. One of the pictures was of a ferocious-looking oriental gentleman mounted on a hardy little pony.

'That's a grand wee horse,' muttered McCann, out of the side of his mouth. 'I wonder who's your man?' She heard but for some reason she was more inclined to purr than scratch that afternoon.

'That's Genghis Khan,' she told us.

I can think of no good reason why the activities of that faraway Mongol chieftain should have been remotely interesting to a horde of spotty children in a village school on the other side of the globe. The Fearful Fogarty One perhaps yearned for those distant days when you could bombard your enemies with the severed heads of their friends as an encouragement to toe the line. Whatever the reason, that afternoon we had an extempore, general knowledge lesson on Genghis Khan.

'He was some fella, that Genghis,' said McCann to me as we dawdled past Felix Mullin's saddler's shop after school. At that very moment, Felix came out of the shop and asked us to deliver a football he had repaired to a house on our way home.

We idly booted the ball before us along the road and I listened with half an ear to McCann enthusing about the Khan, or more exactly, the grand wee horses he had in such abundance. I was thinking of the local sports meeting that weekend, and of the goal-scoring competition in particular.

'Why don't we go in for the goal-scoring competition?' I said to McCann.

'Is your head away?' he said, still in Mongolia with the wonderful ponies. 'What do we know about goal-scoring?'

Where football was concerned, it's true, we were a pair of no-hopers, but I had been getting some coaching on the art and inner mystery of the drop-kick.

'The secret's in the drop-kick,' I said, airily. 'It's easy. Brendan taught me.'

This was a lie. My brother had tried to impart some of his mastery to me and had failed completely. Nonetheless I expounded on the theory of those low, powerful, curving shots that fooled goalkeepers. I gave the impression that the technique of kicking the ball at the precise instant it touched the ground was second nature to me.

'Like this?' said McCann and dropped the ball.

It was a perfect drop-kick. It was a fluke but it was perfect. His boot connected with the ball at the exact moment the ball touched the ground. The resulting shot, low and beautiful to behold, rose with deceptive ease right above the centre of the road. As we watched in breathless admiration, the Fearful Fogarty One came over a gentle rise in the road on her bike and down towards us. She had no business being there. The village and the school lay in the opposite direction. The road led only to the edge of the Moyola river and the river was crossed only by a narrow wooden footbridge, known inexplicably as the Iron Bridge. Being in the wrong place at the right time was only one of her numerous and undesirable gifts.

The events of the next few seconds are graven forever on my mind. Like a ball-bearing leaving a catapult, the football travelled right between the handlebars and took her amidships. It seemed to carry her backwards off the saddle, while the bike sailed majestically on for several yards before tilting, ticking gently, into the ditch. She hung in mid-air for a millisecond and then thudded to the ground.

With one mighty leap we were over the hedge and into McNeill's meadow. Considering the speed with which it had all happened, it should have simply been a matter of the detailed preparation of bare-faced lies for Monday morning. Given the advantage of surprise in our favour we should have escaped, except that McCann threw himself down on the spongy grass of the meadow. He rolled over on his back and howled with monstrous, unholy joy. Huge, rib-stretching gusts of laughter shook his frame. Tears of hilarity coursed down his cheeks.

'Get up,' I urged frantically. 'We'll be caught.'

'Ah, to hell with her,' yodelled McCann (once again I have cleaned up his utterance) and he kicked his heels in the air, miming a cyclist apparently crossing a ceiling. I fell beside him on the grass and even after all these years I can still clearly recall the pair of us rolling and screaming with laughter as she arrived in our midst. She had entered the meadow in more orthodox fashion, by the gate, and, incongruously, carried the ball under her arm.

On Monday morning she thrashed seven bells out of us but it hardly mattered. By that time we were famous. As we trudged back to our desks, our tingling hands clenched under our armpits, Andy Boyle, who could nearly match us scar for scar inflicted by the Fearful Fogarty One, tapped the picture of Genghis Khan.

'Good on you, Genghis,' he said to McCann, in a loud stage whisper. A tidal wave of laughter washed over the room. Mutinous and demoralising, it turned the tide in our favour. Half an hour later Jim Gunn put his head round the door, announced he was coming back the following morning, and was greeted with tumultuous cheering. He didn't know it then, but he had just missed the birth of a legend.

9 The Ceili House

There was a man in our part of the world who made a profitable sideline out of a wheelbarrow. It was a bit before my time, but I can remember the details because I was young and impressionable and I had mastered the art of keeping a low profile when the ceiliers came in.

Aunt Mary's house had the reputation of being a good ceili house and on any night of the week, winter or summer, there might be as many as a dozen neighbours in the kitchen, yarning and reminiscing. Of course I wanted to hear all this, but Aunt Mary took the view that a lot of it wouldn't be in my best interests, so if I did anything to draw her attention to me I might find myself shunted off to bed.

And then I wouldn't have heard about Old Harry and the wheelbarrow. There was some disagreement among the ceiliers about the actual number of wheelbarrows involved, but the man who had the last word insisted that there was only one. Old Harry made this wheelbarrow to order for a neighbour, painted it red, delivered it and collected his money. Some time later another neighbour saw the handsome new barrow, admired it and engaged Old Harry to make him one. Harry carried out the work at impressive speed and in a matter of days the new customer had a spanking new barrow, painted blue.

The customer was delighted with his purchase, and sympathetic when the owner of the red barrow reported that his new one had been stolen. Blame was allotted to the gypsies, the police were informed and the aggrieved one placed another order with Harry. After a decent interval a nice brown barrow was handed over, round about the time the gypsies were accused of making a return visit and making off with the second man's blue barrow. The poor gypsies were fair game for anything, and Old Harry was long retired from the manufacturing business before the owner of the brown barrow, carrying out a minor repair to it, stumbled on the truth. Beneath the brown paint there was a coat of blue and below that one of red and below that . . . well, you've got the picture.

This particular barrow had been sold, stolen back, resold, stolen again, nobody knew how many times. And nobody knew how many barrows Harry had actually made and put through

this process. He was able to retire early, though not on his
ill-gotten gains from the wheelbarrow industry. He had been the
youngest of a very large family in which the first had died in
infancy. When he was christened his parents, whether from
reasons of sentiment or lack of imagination, had named him after
the one who had died. He had, it seems, used the dead one's date
of birth to claim the pension years before his own was due. Of
course, reasoned the ceiliers, what could you expect from a man
who had tacked his own surname after that of his collie bitch
Nellie and wangled an extra ration book for himself during the
war?

Somewhere in the midst of all this humorous reminiscing there
may have been a grain of truth, buried in the distant past. In
South Derry, as everywhere else, things lost nothing in telling. I
remember Neil Mullin's reaction to that story. He had been
sitting reflectively smoking his pipe with a slightly whimsical
smile on his broad, lined face.

'There was a man in Glenelly one time,' he said, 'away back
when I was a youngster, and he took a terrible fit of coughing.
After a while he took to his bed, still coughing away and the
neighbours started to wonder what was wrong with him. Then
one day somebody went up to the house and asked his wife what
was the matter with him, and when he was coming back down
the road he met another neighbour and the chat came round
about the man who was doing all the coughing.'

Neil leaned over and spat copiously into the fire.

'Well, the man who had been up at the cougher's house put a
long face on him and said, "I don't think Mick – that was the
cougher's name – is going to do".'

If you weren't 'going to do' you were about to die, in the local
dialect.

'Lord bless us and save us,' said the other man. 'What's wrong
with him?'

'Oh,' said the first man, 'the wife told me he coughed up a
crow.'

'Namea God,' the second man said, 'how could a crow have got
into him?'

'Well,' said the first man, 'there's you and there's it, and I have
to be going.' And off the two of them went, in different directions, to spread the good news that there would soon be a wake to
go to and by the afternoon everybody had rehearsed all the nice
things they were going to say about Mick, how he was a decent
man, and never did anybody a bad turn, and all the usual
compliments they wouldn't have used the day before.

Between the two of them they managed to increase the number
of crows Mick had coughed up to a total of seven by nightfall and
the district was in a fine state of excitement about the whole

business. The next morning, to everybody's intense disappointment, Mick was seen out in one of his fields, vigorously digging a
drain, and a deputation of neighbours called on him to explain
about the crows, for one thing, and why he had deprived them of
a wake for another.

'What's all this blether about crows?' Mick demanded, very
crossly. 'I coughed up something as black as a crow, that's all.'

The deputation assumed delighted expressions at his miracu-
lous deliverance.

'And do you know what it was?' the patient demanded of his
audience, to remove any lingering doubts from their minds that
he was suffering from something sinister. 'A bit of a burnt scone,'
he told them. 'That bloody woman's bad baking will be the death
of me yet.'

The ceiliers shifted a bit on their chairs, before they laughed a
trifle self-consciously and turned to more mundane topics like
potato blight. Neil could make his points tactfully.

He was a stonemason by trade and although he was past
middle age when I knew him, he had been considered an eligible
bachelor in his younger days. This guaranteed him an active
social life for he was welcome in a lot of houses with marriageable
daughters to dispose of. They were naturally anxious to demonstrate their culinary skills, and so Neil enjoyed a higher standard
of living than many of his contemporaries. He reasoned, probably with some justification, that the standard of cuisine might
fall if he took the matrimonial plunge.

When a local farmer engaged Neil to build a barn, he spent a
good deal of time extolling the virtues of his three daughters,
slowing up the progress of building, to the builder's polite
annoyance.

'You've convinced me,' Neil said, after a particularly lengthy
eulogy. 'I'll take two.'

He took none of all the offers and was found dead, of natural
causes, in his lonely bed shortly after the war ended, but they tell
his stories around Draperstown still.

There seems to have been a proliferation of elderly bachelors
around the district, many of them with delusions about their
marital eligibility. I remember Andy particularly well for his
cheque-book gimmick. He always found some excuse for dropping it, preferably in the vicinity of a likely bride, but failing that,
anywhere it could be seen, regardless of the audience. Any
publicity was good publicity in his view, and the more people
speculated about his wealth and substance, the higher his standing was in the community.

Apart from his almost eerie lack of personality, however, Andy
suffered from a number of disadvantages. He had three un-
married sisters and a bachelor brother. The cheque book may

have represented a cash value of tens, or thousands, but the gamble of finding out, when compounded by the additional odds of the three sisters, was more than any woman would have risked.

Henry, the other brother, had no illusions about his eligibility, or if he had, he never mentioned them in the ceili houses. His chief affectation was to imagine that their farm, though in reality not much bigger than anyone else's, was so vast that he could never remember, to within the nearest 10, the number of cattle they owned. Every so often, then, he would set out to count them, a job which might have taken 15 minutes for anyone else but which he managed to stretch out over an entire Sunday afternoon. He chose Sunday afternoons for the head count because people out for a stroll would meet him and be told he couldn't rest until he had established the number. The tally was usually 35, or maybe 36. At any rate marginally higher than the average number for the district and enough for disrespectful youngsters speeding past on their bikes and, taking their cue from their elders, to yell 'How many have you today, Henry?'

Henry took this kind of irreverence stoically and put it down to falling modern standards of respect for one's elders and betters. The brothers' pride in their possessions was really a harmless thing and there was no malice in the amusement it generated.

Matt Rogers was a regular ceilier in Aunt Mary's house and I particularly enjoyed his contributions to the discussions. He came from a townland on the farthest boundary of the parish that seemed to be home to a wider variety of characters than we had closer to hand. Matt's storytelling skills certainly made them seem different. He had a neighbour called Tom McFadden who had a name for being very protective about money. Any that got into his clutches escaped only with the greatest difficulty. It happened one year that McFadden's potato crop had been condemned by the agricultural inspector, who ordered him to start from scratch again with new seed. This development, according to Matt, was entirely due to McFadden's stinginess with fertilisers.

'May the devil rub it into him,' Matt said with relish, for he was a man who had no time for meanness. He was good for a secretive sixpence every time he came, so he got my vote.

'Well, anyway,' Matt went on, 'I was the only man about that had a ton of seed to spare and the deal was made for 20 pounds. And that took most of the day, too. He must have wanted them for nothing. Sure any of the merchants would pay me that much anyway.'

He paused for dramatic effect.

'He took them away yesterday evening,' Matt said. 'I was shaving in the kitchen when he came in to pay me for them.

He threw down the three fivers ready enough, then he got down
to the pound notes. He put one down and looked at me but I
never let on. I just went on shaving. He threw down another one
and he looked at me a bit harder. I never bothered. He put
another one down and I thought he was going to take a weak
turn.'

'Eighteen down, two to go,' said one of the company.

'Right,' said Matt. 'Then he produced the 10-bob notes. Two of
them, rolled up into wee balls. He smoothed them out, and he set
one down, and he put his face so close to me I nearly cut him.
"Keep going, Tom," says I.'

'He wanted a good luck penny,' somebody remarked. It was
the local custom to give discount on a deal, for luck. There would
be no question, in the ordinary way, of looking for a luck penny of
30 shillings, but Tom's way of looking at financial matters wasn't
ordinary.

'He gave me the other one,' Matt said. 'Then he got down to the
small change, half-crowns, two bob bits, tanners, threepenny
bits, pennies, he thought I wasn't counting but there was 19
pounds, 19 shillings and sixpence on that table and he was as
white as a sheet. "You're a tanner short, Tom," says I.'

The ceiliers guffawed their appreciation.

'Well, boys, he threw that tanner down so hard it rolled off the
table and across the floor, and he nearly took the door off its
hinges going out. I picked it up, and do you know what?'

Matt paused again. The company eyed him expectantly, the
beginnings of a smile hovering on every lip.

'The track of his thumbnail was on it,' Matt finished
triumphantly. 'Here, young fella, see for yourself,' and he
flipped a sixpence across to me.

There was no mark on the coin. I exchanged it for two ice-
creams in O'Kane's shop the next day at lunch-time.

The visit of the thresher was a seasonal topic of conversation in
the ceili houses, and gave rise to discussion under three main
headings. Yield of corn, total of rats killed by various dogs and
the banter exchanged between the various wits at each farm. No
money changed hands during the threshing season except to the
owner of the machine. All labour was provided on an exchange
basis but it was understood that the food would be nourishing
and plentiful.

This hope wasn't always realised and Matt achieved a measure
of fame on one occasion when the only extra item to appear on the
table was a dish of honey. It was ignored by the assembled
farmers who devoted their attention to farming matters for most
of the meal-break. The inevitable lull occurred, and Matt chose
this moment to dip his knife in the honey, raise it and study the
golden product with the air of a connoisseur. He repeated the

performance until he had the undivided attention of the assembled farmers.

'I notice, Mrs Murphy,' he said, very deliberately, 'that you
keep a bee.'

There was always a certain amount of rivalry between farmers'
wives on the subject of cookery generally, but in particular
baking, butter-making and egg production. Aunt Mary excelled
at all these and could afford to keep a tolerant silence when they
came up during ceilis. One farmer's wife, having been defeated
by another's argument that there was a detectable difference in
taste and quality between brown eggs and white ones, evolved a
theory that the same would apply to butter.

In the effort to prove this point she drove everyone on the farm
close to insanity. There were black cows, brown cows and white
cows on the farm and in pursuit of her theory she had their milk
churned separately. Churning was a monotonous task, and hard
work as well, but when the effort was trebled for the same
output, tempers reached breaking point. The work was only part
of it. The product had to be tasted, too. The butter was set out in
different dishes at meal-times and everyone at the table was
requested to identify which butter originated from which cow.

They always made an effort, but all they could produce was
guesswork complicated by their raging apathy, and the results
weren't pleasing to the lady. Any idiot could tell the difference,
she stormed, but no idiot was ever made smarter by being
shouted at, or more co-operative, either.

Then one day Frank McGlade turned up at the farm to give a
hand and found himself roped in as a taster. He was told that each
dish contained a different cow's product but not which dish was
which. He was invited to take his time, butter a piece of bread
from each dish, and give his verdict at his leisure. He carried out
the instructions, deadpan and to the letter. Then he identified
one dish of butter as originating from the black cows. He was
right and the lady was delighted, not only at the discovery of such
a sophisticated palate, but at the vindication of her theory.

'How did you know?' she asked, as soon as she could control
her excitement.

'There's black hairs in it,' said Frank, seizing his cap and
making for the great outdoors.

The verdict brought the lunacy to an end and it brought the
local optician a turn of business, too. It also brought a certain
coolness into the domestic scene, as Matt pointed out, but no
matter, for as Flann O'Brien once remarked, in another context, it
was good for the telling. And a great line to finish a night's ceili
on, too.

10 *St Columb's*

I arrived at St Columb's College in Derry in a somewhat confused state of mind. My experience of school was limited to Draperstown Public Elementary School and in spite of the many questions I had asked, had formed no clear picture of how a grammar school worked.

Malachy had already been there for three years but on several important points his description of the place fell short of ideal. My father had obtained an undertaking from him that he would see that I did my work, but I couldn't see how he could possibly deliver. He had already told me about different classes and different teachers for different subjects and people on the move from room to room every 40 minutes, so how he was going to keep an eye on me was a mystery. Under Jim Gunn's regime there had been no homework. He reasoned it was a waste of time and had preferred to concentrate on written and practical classwork, and so I figured that all schools must operate on the same principle.

The mystery was simply explained. St Columb's operated on a large-scale homework basis. Home, unless you were a day-boy, was interpreted in this case as the study hall, which opened for business at five o'clock in the afternoon and closed down at 10. There was a break of 10 minutes at 25 past six and another from half-past seven until half-past eight. This regime, under the vigilant supervision of teachers on a rota, operated seven nights a week. Plus an extra hour on Sunday mornings if the weather was wet. And it mostly was.

Juniors, those in their first three years, had their own study hall, though if they had brothers in the senior years, they were required to spend the study hours in the senior study hall sitting beside the big brothers. Thus the college extended its authority through the family network, and probably had been doing so long before Orwell dreamed up his Big Brother theory. All this enlightenment was in the future when I first stepped off the bus inside the college gates.

The college drew its pupils from Donegal, Fermanagh, and County Derry, as well as a huge day-boy contingent from the city itself. The South Derry pupils were numerous enough to merit a special bus.

St Columb's didn't fit the popular concept of a boarding school in every way. There were dormitories, of course, but people who had brothers were allocated bedrooms, which were big enough to be shared by as many as four. In this case each one had a wrought-iron wash-stand with enamel basin and jug. You collected a jug of water each night from one of the bathrooms on each floor. There was no nonsense about hot water for washing. All beds had to be stripped each morning as soon as you got up, and remade after breakfast. This came as a serious shock to lads whose doting mammies had made their beds for them.

Not, I fancy, as big a shock as when they sat down for their first meal in the college dining hall, known as the refectory. This was merely an official title. It had other names among the diners. The refectory was terrazzo-floored and seated about 240 people. The first time a newcomer heard 960 chair-legs being dragged back over terrazzo the very instant the last word of Grace was uttered knew what it must have been like to have been a resident of Pompeii at the wrong moment in history.

The first meal of the term was supper, which was also the last meal of each day, anyway. It consisted of tea, bread, butter and jam. The tables seated either 10 or 15, catered for in groups of five. There was a loaf for five, a pot of tea for five, a dish of jam for five. The butter was served on each plate, in scrupulously fair portions. Everybody got two, about the diameter of 10-pence pieces and twice as thick, machine produced. Of course, the stuff wasn't butter.

Sometimes the teapots would spray out tea like a demented fire hydrant, sometimes they permitted only the occasional dribble to emerge from around the lid. If you could coax it out of the pot it was wet and warm, and there its resemblance to tea ended. The bread wasn't sliced and the back of the breadknife was often sharper than the edge. It was in coping with the unsliced loaf that the boarder came into his own. It took skill and concentration to divide such a loaf into 10 slices. And it had to be 10. Nine and somebody only got one. Eleven and somebody got three. That was a recipe for mutiny.

A subtle assessment took place on the first evening of each year. Permanent places were allocated on the second day but it was a kind of free-for-all at the first supper. Old hands would graciously permit a new boy to slice the loaf. Well fed after two months at home, they could afford to be indulgent just this once. If the new boy should betray his amateurishness by producing pyramid-shaped slices he was immediately marked down as a lad who had his bread, and possibly meat, cut up for him at home. Such a boy, reasoned the old campaigners, would have a doting mother who at the moment was stifling her tears as she cooked chickens and baked cakes to send in bulging food parcels to her starving offspring. And such a boy, in spite of the abuse heaped on his head, would never be short of help to consume to the aforementioned cakes and chickens.

The next meal was breakfast. It differed from supper in that only one piece of butter was served and there was no jam. To compensate there was porridge. Sometimes you could drink it, occasionally you could chew it, but it had one constant element. Lumps. Pupils of a scientific bent claimed that they had been specially made years before and were used over and over again, on the principle of Archimedes, to reduce the space available for more nourishing contents. This was contested by historically inclined pupils, who maintained that they were leftover ammunition from the unpleasantness between William and James some centuries before.

Between breakfast and dinner there was lunch, a curious affair that has coloured my attitude to the midday collation ever since. It consisted of tea, in the inevitable eccentric teapot, and a slice of either bread-and-jam (no butter) or fried bread. For this repast the kitchen staff had an endless supply of loaves consisting entirely of heels of varying thickness but uniform hardness. The ration was one of these delicacies per person. On the days when they were fried rather than jammed, the frying was carried out around mid-morning, or perhaps the day before. It was possible to squeeze large globules of congealed grease from cracks in the surface and listen to them hit the table with sounds varying from a plop to a thud. Wisely perhaps, no Grace was said before or after this repast.

The main meal of the day was dinner. 'Is it true,' a day-boy once asked me,' that they give you little titbits to whet your appetite, you know, horses' dofors, as the French say?' He fled before I could decapitate him. Unlike the boarders whose days and nights were regimented in every detail, day-boys had an active social life, and where food was concerned this could be turned to advantage.

Boarders, having no other way of passing their evenings except in study, very often developed a commercially viable expertise in academic matters. Day-boys, being free to go the pictures, chase girls and indulge in similar diversions, often found themselves short of, say, a page or two of French translation. A trading position developed, in which corned beef sandwiches, which the day-boys seemed to mine in large quantities, could be exchanged for a given amount of French translation. The rate fluctuated. If there was a carnival going on anywhere in the Inishowen peninsula the rate could go through the roof. There were other times when academic expertise was a glut on the market.

The quality of dinner remained fixed at poor. Two or three hundred teenagers with hollow legs in the last days of post-war rationing could be controlled only by strict discipline, plenty of work and a divide-and-rule policy. For example, things like potatoes had to be in multiples of five so that 10 in a dish meant two each. Of course, one or two of them might be bad, and indeed on a bad day the lot might be inedible. The number, however, was always either nine or 11. Equitable distribution was achieved, as soon as permanent places were allocated, by spinning a knife flat on the table. When it stopped spinning, the person it was pointing at was designated First Extra. Going in a clockwise direction, the next was second and so on. The numbers were rotated on a daily basis to ensure fair play. By this primitive means the knavish tricks of the ruling class were thwarted.

There was always plenty of cabbage both with and after the meal, for it topped no one's hit parade of foods. Meatballs of varying sizes (but never in multiples of five) predominated on the menu, and tapioca, known as frog spawn, seemed invariably to bring the meal to an end.

Curiously enough nobody ever asked for more. But then, to the best of my recollection, *Oliver Twist* was the only Dickens novel not on the syllabus during my time at the school.

A small field ran along one side of the school grounds, separated from a couple of football pitches by a path and a hedge that had vanished in several places, trodden into nothingness by generations of pupils in pursuit of stray balls. The field was out of bounds, naturally, and each successive principal had reinforced the ban, in the belief that his edict would be much cheaper than a hedge. The owners of the field had a touching faith in the principal's authority, so they kept hens there.

One sunny afternoon a few of us were sprawling languidly on a high bank overlooking the field when one boy mentioned, in some detail, how much he would enjoy a leg or two of chicken. Another in the group pointed at the hens and challenged him to satisfy his craving. In a flash he was into the field and stalking his prey through the long grass, his crew-cut head barely visible. The poor hen never knew what hit her. One minute she was happily pecking her way through life without a care, the next her neck was several inches longer and her feathers were flying in all directions. Our man, it transpired, had earned a crust or two the previous Christmas plucking turkeys for a dealer.

The thing was by no means as spontaneous as I thought, and he cleaned and cooked the bird as well. He had filched a basic methylated-spirit stove from a science lab and a saucepan from the kitchens, and he entered a nearby classroom block through a window and cooked the carcass there. To remove things from the lab was a hanging offence and to be discovered in the kitchens without permission, never mind stealing things from there, would have added quartering to the punishment. He offered us all a share of the feast but we left it all to himself and asked no questions as to how he had disposed of the evidence.

The kitchens weren't out of bounds because of the secret, gourmet recipes prepared there, but because they were staffed by maids and therefore a source of serious temptation, though temptation to what wasn't clear. It was even an offence to speak to any of the maids. The usual effect of prohibitions is to make people do the opposite but I can't recall a single instance of anyone getting into trouble for speaking to a maid. Of course the college authorities had hedged their bets a bit by being suitably careful in their selection of domestic staff.

The was another source of food, especially for those who had money. The Southend fish-and-chip shop farther down Bishop Street was, naturally, out of bounds, which made it very attractive. The easy way to get to it was straight out through the front gate, but leaving the grounds without permission was a serious offence and the gate was in full view of both the principal's and dean's offices.

My favourite point of exit was via the branch of an oak tree that overhung the grounds of a primary school in Bishop Street. They closed their gate, a dangerous, spiked affair, at the close of business each day while ours was kept sadistically open. Once out in the street it was simply a matter of marching briskly past our own gate. The young and impressionable tended to be a bit furtive at first but then the young and impressionable didn't often make the journey. One or two trips turned them into hardened sinners.

The people who lived opposite the primary school must have been frequently entertained by seeing up to a dozen fish suppers handed over the gate of an empty school into disembodied hands, to be followed by the carrier moving at something approaching the speed of light. It was an understood thing that only one carrier made the trip. This minimised the risk of large-scale retribution and it also meant that the carrier didn't need to have money of his own. He was paid in the form of a levy on each subscriber. I have reason to know that a daring operator could live quite well at the expense of more timorous but equally hungry colleagues. I can still smell those chips from the Southend in my mind's nose and as the years pass I sometimes wonder why I can never get chips like that any more.

The answer, like my nose, is right in front of me. Like the man who travelled the world in search of pancakes as good as his mother used to make, I no longer have the stomach I had then. Well, actually, I have more of it but its uncritical digestive properties are not what they were all those autumns ago, when a paragraph of Victor Hugo was worth a sandwich in the Maiden City.

11   *Transition*

The grammar school course in the 1950s was five years long. At the end of the third year came the junior certificate, a public examination in the domain of the Ministry of Education. I suppose it would have been the equivalent of O-levels. Your fate depended on your performance at this stage. It you passed a junior subject with distinction you could go on to take it at A-level in the senior certificate two years later.

There was no codology about taking a subject at O-level first. If you just got a credit you went on to take it at O-level. It was either one or the other. If you merely passed a subject your fate hung in the balance. If you had enough passes of sufficiently low marks you might be asked to leave. It wasn't necessary to fail a lot of subjects in order to be shown the door.

A kind of continuous assessment operated. At the end of each term examinations were set and the results supplied to parents, along with comments on both academic performance and behaviour. It was frequently necessary for me to intercept these reports – they always arrived during the holidays – and either make suitable amendments or post them in the fire. For my first three years this was quite difficult since two reports arrived together, one for me and one for Malachy. Speed was of the essence if bad news had to be kept from my father. A certain amount of time was needed to tailor a report, and time wasn't always on my side, especially since his never needed any kind of amendment. There were very few grammar school pupils around Drumderg in the '50s and by some mysterious, bush telegraph system, news of the reports was in circulation the very day they arrived, and sometimes the day before.

The first examination I recall doing was of the mathematical variety, a subject I have viewed with undisguised loathing ever since. I remember one question from that paper, and with good reason. It concerned a bath which was allegedly filling with water from two taps. I say 'allegedly' because this bath had sprung a leak, so that the water was escaping almost as fast as taps A and B were filling it. To further complicate the issue, the taps were delivering different amounts and at different speeds.

The person who had devised this question wanted to known how long it would take for the bath to fill. At the age of 12 I was almost as cynical as I am now about the motives of people who frame and inflict examination questions. Turning to the candidate sitting nearest me I passed a derisory comment on the half-wit who had concocted this rigmarole. I turned back to my task just in time to collide with a fist travelling towards my jaw from the opposite direction. It belonged to the teacher supervising the exam who also happened to be the framer and perpetrator of that question. I failed that exam. A judicious alteration of the report when it came kept this calamitous news from my father.

The quality of teaching varied wildly. St Columb's had been established originally as a junior diocesan seminary with the object of providing a secondary education for boys intending to go on to the major seminaries like Maynooth to train for the priesthood. The qualifying examination changed all that. Although a substantial number of pupils were aiming for the religious life, the vast majority of the Eleven Plus intakes had different ambitions.

About half the staff were priests who lived on the premises. None of them had taken holy orders with a view to becoming teachers but the bishop thought otherwise and appointed them to the teaching staff according to their degrees. Several years would have passed between the time they took their degrees and their arrival at St Columb's, the intervening time having been spent mastering the complexities of theology. They had one thing in common with their lay colleagues. None of them had any teacher-training. This isn't always a bad thing. The chief merit of teacher-training is that it alerts teachers to how little they know about the needs of the consumer. There are some, though not many, who are born with that insight, and St Columb's happened to have employed a few of them, more by luck than anything else.

My own career brought me into contact with the entire range of teaching talent. A brief flirtation with chemistry ended when a new teacher, a Corkman with a ferocious temper, concluded that that the message could best be driven home with the rubber tubing of a Bunsen burner. He departed after a year but I had abandoned the subject long before.

On the other hand, virtually all of my mathematical knowledge was gained in my third year when I found myself in Father Martin Gildea's class. He could simplify the most complex ideas by using a system of mnemonics he had devised himself. Even yet, whenever I see 'OHMS' on an envelope I remember that opposite over hypotenuse means sine. He would frequently enliven proceedings by bursting into song, telling a yarn, reading us an extract from some detective story that took his fancy or even executing a few dance steps on the podium. His ebullient character contrasted starkly with the negative personalities of some of his colleagues and the thuggery of others. Our acquaintance lasted, unfortunately, just the one year.

My love of history can be easily traced to Jack Gallagher, known for some reason as Rusty. He taught us the first year of the A-level course. First impressions were of a stern, precise man but this was misleading. He was a droll character with a keen insight into the teenage personality and an instinct for saying the right thing. He encouraged us to look behind the bald facts of history, to examine causes and identify effects. He was the only history teacher I've ever met who had a total disregard for the importance of dates. At the start of the second year an internal shake-up delivered us into the hands of another teacher who prepared us for a major exam by making us learn the set texts off by heart. I don't know what the rest of my classmates thought, but privately I stuck to the Rusty Gallagher method, and it got me the A-level.

My English teacher for much of my time was Father James Coulter. He was small, neat and amiable-looking, but far from amiable in one important respect. He had no time for fools or chancers, whether in the school, in his classes or in the world outside.

'What's your name, boy?' he demanded of me one day after I had been in his class for several years. A hush fell over the class. This was his invariable preliminary to a dressing-down, for he knew everyone in the school from the day they arrived. It was a trick question. If you gave your surname, he would ask for your Christian name. If you began with your Christian name he would sharply inform you that he had no wish to know it.

'Kelly,' I replied tentatively.

'Your first name?' he snapped.

'Owen,' I answered, preparing for the worst.

'Owen Kelly,' he said, thoughtfully. 'I have only come across that name once in Irish history. He was a farm labourer in the early 1800s.' He was not a great fan of the farming community.

'In the Limavady region, I believe,' he continued. 'He was hanged.'

Something in his manner suggested that not nearly enough people were being hanged.

'For shooting the landlord,' he finished.

There are times when the right response springs unbidden to the lips and in my case they're not often but to my surprise I heard myself say 'Was the landlord called Coulter?'

The furniture in that room was ancient and creaky but not a single creak broke the silence. The class, whose collective heads had been swinging back and forth Wimbledon-style, focused unblinkingly on the Reverend James Coulter. A fool had rushed in where angels wouldn't have gone without an escort. He leaned back in his chair and his shoulders began to shake. With mirth, not rage. He tilted the chair farther back, put his feet up on the front desk and chortled with delight. After a decent pause to make sure it was safe to do so, the class dutifully joined in. From that day forth I could do no wrong.

My last year at school was respectable, uneventful and cost a lot of my fellow pupils money in lost bets. There was a tradition in the school called the Lists. On the first Sunday of each year the entire school would assemble in the chapel, and the principal would read the rules and announce the list of prefects. There were 10 of these functionaries, all final year pupils, all enjoying considerable authority and quite a few privileges. For example, a request to go out to the pictures on a Saturday afternoon was always granted to a prefect and automatically denied to everyone else.

In the first days of the year, therefore, the gamble was to predict the correct 10 candidates. You submitted your 10 choices and a shilling bet to one of the self-appointed bookies and an all-correct forecast earned you 10 shillings.

Every year one or two punters would come up with a correct list but there were no winners in my last year. The first eight or nine were reasonably predictable and there was a certain hopeful restlessness among the congregation as the principal folded up his notes before delivering himself of the last name.

'Library prefect, Owen Kelly,' he said and walked out.

If he had announced the excommunication of the entire school he couldn't have got a more stunned reaction. Your man Kelly, him that got thrown out twice and kept back that Hallowe'en? The fellow that was caught coming out of the Strand cinema with a girl from Thornhill one Saturday last year? Nobody was more stunned than I was. It took us all quite a while, and me longer than most, to spot that what the man was doing was turning a poacher into a gamekeeper. I met Father Coulter in the corridor a few minutes later. He gave me a conspiratorial wink. 'Some people just have to be saved from themselves,' he said enigmatically and passed on.

This shrewd appointment didn't have any appreciable effect on anybody's behaviour except my own. I suppose the principal thought that to take one setter of bad example out of circulation was bonus enough for the school. Of course I never once failed to apply to the dean for permission to go to the pictures on Saturdays but I have to admit that the crack had gone out of it entirely.

There wasn't much excitement in rambling through the city knowing that I had every right to be there. I even contemplated admitting to the dean that I had borrowed his bike for a visit to Creggan during the previous year, just to see what his reaction would be. After due consideration I abandoned the idea. There's a limit to the extent you can test people's endurance and live to talk about it.

The examination timetable for that year meant that I was one of the last half-dozen still in residence at the end of the following June. When I walked out into Bishop Street for the last time I saw one of the lay teachers approaching on the far side and I particularly wanted a word with him. Now that it was safe to do so, I wanted to ask why he hadn't reported me the year before when he saw me coming out of the Strand Cinema with the girl from Thornhill, at a time when I was supposed to be in the college attending to my studies. Before I drew level somebody on the other side stopped to talk to him and he didn't see me pass. And that's how my grammar school career ended. Not with a bang, not even with a whimper.

As far as my father was concerned, my arrival home increased the work-force on the farm by one. The first thing he sent me to do was help my Uncle Barney with a fencing job. His cattle, it seemed, had decided that the young corn on the other side of the hedge was more to their taste than the grass they were eating. It goes to show how desperate the situation was for Barney to ask for my help.

We set off, on my first post-school day, with a variety of fencing tools to make good the hedge. I use the word good advisedly, for when the uncle fixed something, it stayed fixed. Well, we fixed that hedge and I can say with pride that it would have withstood a cavalry charge. We had time in hand when we finished so he decided it was an ideal moment to replace a rotting fence post. It should have been a simple operation.

Barney held the new post in position and indicated that I should strike it authoritatively with the seven-pound sledge hammer. The top of the post was perfectly flat and I aimed a tremendous swipe at it. The hammer connected with the post at the point where the wooden handle entered the head. The handle snapped and the head flew off, buzzing like an angry bee through the space his head had occupied a split second before.

He said nothing in a very pointed manner. He retrieved the two parts of the sledgehammer and in total silence repaired the damage. He removed the remaining pieces of wood from the head, trimmed the end of the handle and joined the bits firmly together again. Lightning does strike twice in the same place. I raised the hammer, I brought it down and I broke it again. He didn't bother to pick up the pieces but you could hear the silence across three parishes. Grasshoppers fled silently to wherever grasshoppers go in moments of stress. Barney lit a cigarette and smoked about half of it. The he launched into a review of my shortcomings.

His tone was measured and he omitted no detail, however insignificant, of the implications of my two attempts to decapitate him. Then he turned to the examinations I had completed the day before and wondered what sort of career awaited me. As far as Barney was concerned, if you were incompetent at one thing you were incompetent at everything. It did not seem the right time to tell him that hedging wasn't part of the syllabus. A man who had twice escaped death in 10 minutes at the hands of a blood relative he had never harmed in his life has to be allowed some latitude.

He finished his review by voicing the opinion that it would be a very long time before I would qualify for any profession. Indeed, he added, any profession that would have me in its membership should be banned and its officers submitted to rigorous psychiatric examination. Then he gathered up the tools and we went home.

I would like to say that he was proved totally wrong but with hindsight he may have been right. At the end of the following month I learned that I had been awarded a place at the teacher-training college. It seemed a great idea at the time. Years later I thought there might have been some truth in the final part of his monologue.

12   *Top of the Range*

My father was an acknowledged expert on flax. As a scutcher, and the son of a scutcher this was hardly surprising. His expertise extended beyond the initial processing of his customers' crop. He was also responsible for selling it to the dealers in Cookstown market and his ability to get the last possible penny for their flax earned him the respect of the farmers for whom he acted.

These were men who were expert dealers in their own field, unerring judges of cattle, sheep, pigs or horses. Any animal or standing crop was an open book to them, and to my father as well, for he too was a farmer. Flax, though, was another matter. The buyers who acted on behalf of the linen companies, both home-based and abroad, could visualise the product in a finished state as sheets or tablecloths and therefore had an insight into the fibre's strengths and weaknesses denied to the growers. Selling and buying was an eyeball-to-eyeball confrontation which my father invariably won on behalf of the farmers.

The scutched flax went away in 14 pound greyish bundles and nobody ever saw the process by which it was converted into the expensive, snowy white finished articles. This made my father's heirloom all the more precious. It was a linen tray-cloth made from flax grown on our own farm. From when the seed was sown, to the pulling, retting, drying and scutching, it never left the place. At this point it should have gone away with the rest of the finished crop, but some female ancestor in the 19th century had decreed otherwise. This particular hank of flax stayed, like the little piggy, at home. By dint of perseverance the female ancestor completed the processing, using whatever unsophisticated domestic equipment was available at that time.

The handsomely embroidered tray-cloth never lay on any tray. It lived in a cocoon of tissue paper and my father might on a rare occasion unveil it for a particularly privileged visitor. According to him, the cloth needed to be exposed to the air from time to time, and so it was brought out once or twice a year and spread carefully over a little wooden structure, like a ladder, for its airing. When the ladder wasn't discharging this ritual function, it had the more mundane task of holding the strainer while milk was poured through it into the crocks to await churning.

One hot summer day it fell to me to light the fire in the kitchen range. It says a lot about the manpower shortage on the farm that summer that my father even considered delegating this job to me. I was well known to be incompetent at firelighting, and I had taken care to nurture the image. I had learned at an early age that if you're no good at something, people will first try to show you how it's done and then, if you take a dislike to the task, and look suitably dim-witted, they leave you alone in future.

It was the haymaking season and both Malachy and Brendan were judged to be less dispensable, so I was sent home early to light the fire and start getting the evening meal ready. We had not, at that stage, risen to having a gas cooker. As far as modern household appliances were concerned, my brothers and I were agreed that they would have to be obsolete before my father would discover their merits.

The range, a huge black Stanley 9, was usually lit by the simple expedient of placing a turf in the bottom of the fire-box, and gradually adding fuel as the oil-soaked turf began to burn. The secret was to add the rest of the fuel in small amounts. One block too much and the whole thing went out. On top of the firebox, a series of concentric rings, finishing with a central lid, accommodated the varying diameters of the cooking pots.

I removed all the rings, dropped the oil-soaked turf into the bottom of the firebox and committed the unpardonable offence. I dropped the lit match on top of the turf before I added more fuel. The correct drill, of course, was to set the basic fire, close the top of the firebox and then, but not till then, poke the lit match through the bars from the bottom. In my fit of misplaced efficiency, I had turned aside to pick up some more fuel when from the tail of my eye I saw a tongue of flame shoot through the open top of the firebox and punch a neat hole in something apparently drying on the plate-rack directly above the opening.

I swept the rings and the lid back into place, grabbed the smoking material from the plate-rack and headed for the great outdoors. That jet of flame had transformed me in an instant from a zombie-like teenager to a blur of arms and legs as I moved to prevent the ancestral pile becoming a pile of smoking rubble. It was only when I came to a stop in the middle of the yard that I realised what I was clutching. It was the family heirloom, more precious that the Veil of the Temple. The priceless square of history that the female ancestor had laboured over for countless days and nights now looked like a Mexican poncho.

When a man knows he is to be hanged in the morning, Dr Johnson once remarked, it concentrates his mind wonderfully and even now I wonder at the clarity of my thoughts at that moment. The events of the previous 24 hours passed swiftly before me. The principal of the local school had been a visitor the night before and he and my father had consumed a sufficient

number of bottles of stout for the principal to be considered
worthy to view the priceless cloth.

The viewing coincided with the six-monthly airing ceremony,
so the cloth wasn't returned to its shrine that night. The wooden
frame was fully occupied in its more down-to-earth role, so my
father had spread the cloth over the plate-rack. I had been
delegated to replace it in its wrapping the next day before we left
for the hayfield. As I stood with the smouldering remains in my
hand, I realised that I had forgotten. Suicide seemed like a good
idea. Only my natural cowardice saved me.

There is a divinity that shapes our ends, as Shakespeare said,
no matter how much we may mess them about. At this precise
moment my guardian angel spoke.

'Any old rags?' he asked. I looked round into the unshaven
face, complete with Woodbine, of the ragman.

'I was round this way yesterday and they said they'd leave out
a bag of stuff for me? Is that it?' And he pointed at a sack, neatly
tied, that stood beside the milk-house door.

'I'll just stick this in as well,' I told him and I opened the sack,
shoved the remains of the heirloom down into its packed depths
and retied it, all at the speed of light.

'Do you want a cup or anything?' he asked, in the tones of a
man who wasn't keen about giving one away.

'No, it's all right,' I said and he went away without a word.

The divinity wasn't finished with me. During the rest of my
father's lifetime, a matter of five years, no one of sufficient stature
to be shown the heirloom ever visited us. Even more evidence of
divine protection may be deduced from the fact that the subject of
airing the cloth never came up again either. The fact that it was no
more would never have crossed my father's mind. It was the
unthinkable that saved my life.

Not, however, my conscience. Every time I see or hear expressions like 'top of the range,' or even 'range' in any context, I
react like anyone with a post-hypnotic suggestion planted in their
subconscious. I brace myself and wait for the thunderbolt. From
his better place my father now knows the truth but his priorities
have changed eternally. The time of retribution is perhaps long
past.

13   Called to Higher Things

Back in the 1940s and '50s people still talked in rather grandiose terms about the selection process for admission to teacher-training. People were 'called to training,' an expression with a fine ring to it but little meaning. It was common currency among that section of the community who didn't go out to work, they went out to business instead.

A surprisingly large number of my fellow-pupils applied to become teachers, and one of the reasons originated in our school's attitude to career guidance. There wasn't any. The place had been designed to provide a basic education for aspiring clerics, a profession for whom career guidance would have been an impertinence, since it could be assumed that the Almighty, moving in mysterious ways, would sort out the sheep from the goats without any assistance from mere mortals.

When the government intervened with its scheme for equality of educational opportunity, the college's sacred turf was invaded by all sorts of people with daft notions about all kinds of things and the system didn't know how to cope with these eccentrics. A policy of masterly inactivity ensued, the frequently deplorable results of which are all around us.

The offer of a place in training college came in the form of an invitation for the candidate to present himself for interview, an event surrounded by more horrendous tales than a biography of Dracula. The stories always emanated from somebody who knew somebody whose brother-in-law's nephew or niece had been called and had made a right hames of the whole business. However, I know of only two people who messed up their interviews and one of them did it by not bothering to turn up, and the other startled the panel by informing them that he hated schools, education and all to do with it, and that on no account would he dream of becoming a teacher.

It seems they were going to award him a place anyway, on the grounds that he exhibited the right degree of insanity, but he chose instead to go to Brazil with a construction company. The company survived the experience and flourished, which must prove something but, like the interviews, I'm not sure what.

At my interview I encountered no pitfalls. A slightly built priest, with close-cropped, grey hair and a sallow complexion, sat behind a table flanked by two lesser lay persons. They viewed me in neutral fashion as I came in.

'Mr Kelly?' said the priest. I said nothing, for I assumed the remark was addressed to one or other of the lay henchmen.

'You are Mr Kelly?' the priest repeated quizzically.

I had never been addressed as Mister before and this unexpected elevation to man's estate took me by surprise. I admitted, after a second or two, to being Mr Kelly.

'What have you been doing all summer?' the priest asked politely.

'Pulling flax,' I told him. This was true. After my two failed attempts to decapitate my uncle, I had been hastily recruited back to the family business where, my father seemed to think, I could do little harm.

'Very interesting,' said the priest, alternately studying a sheet of paper and peering at me. 'Have you applied for any other positions?'

'No,' I replied. This wasn't true. I had applied to one or two places but they preferred to wait for examination results. St Mary's Training College had moved first with their offer. A simple 'No,' however, avoided the need for tedious and possibly damaging explanations.

'I think you'll be very happy with us,' the priest said, pushing the sheet back into a folder. 'The rest of the details will be sent to you in due course.' The other two panellists nodded their assent to this searching effort to establish my suitability for the teaching profession.

This was my first meeting with the Rev Dr Patrick Rogers, head of the college. In our many subsequent encounters I was to learn that he was a far shrewder judge of character than my brief and superficial interview might have suggested.

That September I was registered as a student of St Mary's College on the Falls Road, although neither I nor any of my fellow students set foot there except for carefully supervised social functions. For reasons that have never been clear to me, or to anyone else, it was felt necessary to keep male and female students as far apart as possible.

Women students were based in St Mary's itself, some of them living in the college and others in digs or rented accommodation in the vicinity. Men students were trained in Trench House, commonly referred to as The Ranch, a safe distance away, about a mile beyond the trolley-bus terminus at Casement Park. Fraternisation was out, at least during business hours.

Trench House was a free and easy establishment. It was an old country house, home to the Hamill family in bygone years, and the influx of students meant that even the outbuildings had to be converted into makeshift lecture-halls, workshops and laboratories. All students lived away from the college, mostly in digs, though a few of us, myself included, experimented with self-catering accommodation. Not many of us continued the experiments for more than a term.

In those days the banks weren't competing for student business. Banks then clung to the ancient tradition of requiring customers to put money in their accounts before they took it out, so not one of my contemporaries had a bank account. Student grants were in their infancy in the 1950s. They were calculated according to a formula known only to a privileged few in the higher ranks of the civil service and consequently this resulted in some curious anomalies. Two members of the same family pursuing identical courses in the same college might be paid different amounts, for no obvious reason. The paying authorities weren't very trusting either. They made the cheques out to the parents and left the interested parties to sort it out among themselves. In any case they were in no hurry about paying. Each cheque was issued as though it was a layer of skin off the Minister's palm. Payment for the term starting in early September could be as late as November. In fact I once got paid on the eighth of December because some bureaucrat decided I no longer existed. My resurrection took an extra month to prove. By the time the cash arrived virtually all of it was owed to landladies in arrears for digs. These ladies worked on a weekly basis and so became increasingly alarmed as the debts piled up. It even crossed their minds, with good reason on occasion, that their money had gone to support an ailing dog or two at Dunmore Stadium or Celtic Park.

The grant was intended to cover only living expenses. The book allowance was paid separately to the college. In theory any money left over after the purchase of necessary books went to the student at the end of term. In practice most students were in debt to the eyeballs by then and far from the college owing them money, it was generally the other way round. There was a great deal of horse-trading over books and the allowance went on wine, women and song, though not necessarily in that order.

You could get an advance on the allowance, if you had a reasonable excuse. A study of the bursar's records would show that we wore out shoes at an extraordinary rate. It wasn't possible, even in those days, to buy a pair of shoes for two pounds but that was the story most frequently offered to the bursar. Father Eamon McEnaney combined the offices of dean and bursar with his lecturing duties and he was years ahead of his time in his understanding of the financial demands of a student's social life. Eleven o'clock in the morning was the traditional time for students to turn up at his office door with one yarn or another.

Father McEnaney would listen with a disbelieving smile to the student's story, then open the cash box that lived in his desk.

He would write the requested amount down under the student's name in the ledger and push the cash across the desk.

'See you bring that girl home at a decent hour,' he called after one of my friends one morning when negotiations for yet another two-pound pair of shoes had been completed. I thought honesty might be the best policy when I presented myself at his desk.

'I need a quid,' I said, as an opening gambit.

'What for?' he asked.

'Oh, I'm just going to the pictures,' I said.

'By yourself?'

'Well, no, actually. I'm taking a girl.'

'Right,' he said. 'That's two fares into town. Two good seats. I don't want students from this college getting the name of cheap-skates. Two fares home. It can't be done for a pound. You'll need at least two.'

I have no idea what he wrote in the ledger.

It was normal practice to knock on his door and walk straight in. Once in a while Dr Rogers, head of the college, would be found behind the desk and this could lead to unforeseen complications. His approach was different. One student, who was endeavouring to grow a beard, was taken seriously by surprise when he breezed in one morning and found the Doc in command.

'Yes?' he said, taking a close interest in the student's facial fungus.

The student launched into his spiel but found it hard to concentrate under the Doc's penetrating stare. Somehow or other he reached the end of his sob story and waited for results. They weren't what he expected. The Doc stood up, took four pennies from his pocket and pushed them across the desk with a ruler.

'Take these,' he said. 'Go down to McCloskey's shop. Buy a Blue Gillette razor blade. Shave. Closely. Then come back to me after lunch-time and we'll talk finance.'

It was a small college and news spread quickly. When the student came back after lunch-time, clean-shaven, he was met with a chorus of 'Go, show yourself to the priest.'

The Doc wasn't impressed by shoe stories. Another student who unexpectedly found himself dealing with the head of the college stuck to his guns about shoes. The Doc took out his own wallet, produced four one-pound notes and said, 'Get me two pairs while you're about it.'

'Ah, sorry, Dr Rogers,' said the quick-thinking supplicant, 'it's a special offer. Brown suede only.' He departed clutching the two pounds he had asked for. The Doc could be a gracious loser.

I didn't fare so well the time I blundered in and found him in charge. I delivered my request. He looked at his watch.

'Come back in an hour,' he said. 'Your fairy godfather should have returned by then.'

The Doc was a stickler for punctuality and neatness in personal appearance, and frequently expressed his disapproval of the duffle coats that had by then become a sort of student uniform. Overcoats and raincoats of the time were of the dimensions of a Cossack's greatcoat, whereas the duffle coat was a practical garment, cost about three pounds, and it could be slept in if necessary.

He finally accepted duffle coats, I think, the day the first Gannex raincoat appeared in the college. It cost about as much as half-a-dozen duffle coats and was worn by a student who wanted to remind us of his prowess at poker, the selection of fast horses and other pursuits totally unconnected with those the taxpayers thought they were funding. The Doc met him head on in the main hall, which was full of students at the time. He walked all the way round him and stopped.

'Nice,' he said, 'I suppose it cost as much as a real one.'

The way of the innovator can be hard at times.

There were two hot items of news on the Falls Road I particularly remember from that time and one of them concerned the devil. He had appeared at a dance in St Paul's Hall in Hawthorn Street. It seems that a girl at the dance looked down and observed that her partner had a cloven hoof, proof positive, as parents of the time attested, that Old Nick was a regular patron of dance-halls. Naturally she went into hysterics. Whether a hysterical girl could tell the difference between a cloven hoof and a Hughes's bap never entered the heads of those who fuelled the rumour. Nobody knew the girl personally. Everyone knew someone, who knew somebody, who worked with her cousin, and that was nearly as good.

The devil was frightened off by all the publicity and he abandoned St Paul's Hall after his once-only appearance and took up residence in the vicinity of the gates of Milltown Cemetery. This was a much more appropriate location for someone in his line of work and one where he would cause less hysteria among the residents, too. My landlady – for by now I had abandoned my residence in bedsitter-land – used to counsel me to avoid the spot. This was difficult, since all roads home from anywhere interesting led past the gates. We never met in any case.

The other headline-grabbing story was that a girl had been attacked. She was mugged, though the expression hadn't yet arrived in Belfast. The motive was financial, not sexual. Such was the law-abiding atmosphere of the times that the incident was talked about for weeks. The truth was that you could ramble the streets till all hours in those halcyon days and rarely meet anything worse-looking than yourself.

There were rare exceptions, of course. One night as I trudged up the Falls about 20 paces behind a young lady, a fellow on the opposite side of the road crossed towards her with arms out-stretched. She side-stepped adroitly and felled him with a beauti-fully placed blow to the jaw from her handbag. And she didn't even break her step. I formed the impression that it had been a futile attempt at a reconciliation by someone of a suicidal bent. I was relieved when she turned down the Donegall Road and left the Falls entirely to me.

In terms of personal excitement there was the night when I found the dead man lying behind the phone boxes outside the Royal Victoria Hospital, just where the Grosvenor Road joined the Falls. I almost tripped over the body for my mind was on other things. I'll never forget the waxy pallor of the face. I could find no pulse, no sign of life and I had no notion what my next move should be. The need for action was taken out of my hands for an ambulance suddenly turned up the Falls from the Gros-venor and I flagged it down. I knew they'd know what to do. And the ambulance man who got out certainly did.

He eyed the corpse, then grabbed a handful of its shirt with one hand and energetically slapped its face with the other. Life was miraculously restored.

'Get home to hell out of this,' he said. 'You're getting no free taxi tonight.

'He pulls that stroke very Friday night,' he said to me. 'This is the best yet. Usually he comes into casualty to die. He's pretty good at it, too.' He got back into his ambulance and set off in one direction while the ex-corpse took another and I took a third.

Then, there was the torrentially wet night when I was shelter-ing in the doorway of a shop opposite the Falls Baths when a large black car pulled up and a voice offered me a lift. I needed no second invitation, but I was inside before I realised I was in a police car. The policeman who offered me the lift was an ex-St Columb's man, but my landlady, who watched my arrival from her bedroom window, was outraged. What would the neigh-bours think if they saw one of her lodgers being brought home in a police car? I pointed out that it was most unlikely her neigh-bours would be any the wiser, since only policemen and students would be awake or out and about at half-past two in the morning. I got the impression that she would have considered an encoun-ter with Your Man with the Cloven Hoof more socially acceptable.

My landlady was Molly O'Hare, a lady whose formidable exterior and no-nonsense manner concealed the fact that she was one of the kindliest souls who ever lived. It was not surprising that she would have been watching for one of her students to come straggling home in the small hours. Her house in Fruithill

Park was home to an endless procession of students whom she fussed over and fed like prize-fighters.

When one of her flock arrived home soaked to the skin and shivering from playing a football match she ordered him to bed and dosed him with a tumbler of hot whiskey. He protested that he was a Pioneer. She said that she was too but since the prescription was purely medicinal it didn't count.

I've never been a member of that teetotal fraternity, but as far as I know, if a member wants to take a jar for purely medicinal purposes, it must be prescribed by a doctor, otherwise the pledge is broken. Molly disdained such niceties. Her hot whiskey recipe didn't include the addition of any water and she stood over the patient till he drained the tumbler. She always maintained that his subsequent reactions were simply the signs of a fever departing. No one dared suggest that he was splendidly and unmusically drunk for the next 12 hours.

It was a golden, laid-back era, my student days in the 1950s. In spite of the best efforts of the lecturers, teacher-training was an undemanding activity, except for the spells of teaching practice, at which most of us proved to be hopeless. We would have to learn our business the hard way, after we qualified. It was the only practical way.

In the meantime, for two shillings, 10 pence in our modern Monopoly money, you could dance all night in the Orchid on week nights and for half-a-crown you could do the same in Fruithill Club on Sunday nights. We could solve the world's problems over endless cups of coffee in the Continental Café in Castle Street and one night, when I was the last passenger on the bus to Andersonstown from the Floral Hall, the driver said, 'Aw, what the hell,' and drove me right to the door of the digs. Molly rolled her eyes to heaven but conceded that it was better than a police car.

Viewed from the '50s the future was an endless vista of bright tomorrows. The illusion, for all of us, lasted 10 short years.

14 Lost Weekend

Three pounds 10 shillings a week was the student's allowance in the 1950s. No matter what anybody says about the good old days, three-and-a-half quid a week didn't run to a house in leafy suburbia, with manicured lawns and a maid to answer the door. It could, though, be made to stretch to half the rent of a phone-box-sized flat in Belfast's bedsitter-land, with a modest 15 bob or so left over for riotous living. Including food and bus fares, naturally. My generation of students were an abstemious lot.

For the first term I shared a flat with Frank. He was an art student. Even in those days art students looked as if they'd thieved all their clothes off skips. They also have a name for being eccentric in dress and Frank was no exception. He demonstrated his individuality by wearing neat, double-breasted suits, crisp white shirts, gleaming shoes, immaculate ties and a smart gaberdine raincoat if the weather called for it. This was a good ploy.

The first wave of the Eleven Plus generation had reached third-level education. The women students agreed that a degree or diploma was a great thing to have, and a husband with prospects was a useful bonus. Some, indeed, viewed it the other way round, with the qualification as insurance.

Fellows like Frank, with their air of clean-cut reliability, had a great time. His life was as full of girls as a book is of paper. He was tall, dark, with, by all accounts, a great line in blarney and he went home every weekend for a rest. On the other hand, I, being merely tall, was well rested through the week.

The two top floors of the house we lived in were a warren of tiny flats, and the landlady and her family lived on the self-contained ground floor. That place used to empty like magic after breakfast every Friday. Immediately after lectures on Friday afternoons, everybody made for the bus-station or the railway station, with bundles of dirty washing and a week's accumulated appetite. By late evening the residents were scattered all over the province, gorging themselves on home cooking and planning a weekend of what passed for decadence in those distant days.

One weekend I decided to stay over. An obliging dog at Celtic Park had provided me and a few other dissolute souls with the means to do so and the grand finale was to be a Saturday night party. This good fortune wasn't due to any shrewdness on my part, indeed I had never set foot near any dog-track. Tyrone Lass, the winning dog, belonged to a fellow student's uncle who, in a moment of generosity, had tipped off his nephew that he had a sure thing running.

Just how anyone could be sure of anything in the murky world of dog-racing is something one should not enquire too closely into. The nephew shared his inside information with a chosen few, we pooled our meagre resources, he placed the bet and Tyrone Lass flashed home hot on the hare's tail. A rare Saturday night binge seemed appropriate. Easy come, easy go.

I was first in the queue with the rent that Thursday night, and I informed the landlady of my plans. She and her family, it transpired, were also going away that weekend. She wagged a moral finger.

'Now see here, Frank,' she said sternly, 'I don't want you filling the place with girls and such-like when you have the house to yourself.'

'I'm not Frank,' I said, somewhat huffily I admit.

'Oh, that's all right, then,' she said, clearly relieved. 'For the life of me I can't think why I'm always getting you two mixed up.'

I was somewhat superstitious, educationally speaking, and with an exam coming up I decided to forestall the wrath of the examining gods by spending the daylight hours of that Saturday in the library. Not the most exciting way to spend a Saturday, but marginally more attractive than the jobs my father would have lined up for me at home. I reasoned that he would approve of my productive way of spending the day, since I would keep to myself the fact that I had spent the late afternoon and early evening in the Ritz cinema.

It was about eight o'clock when I went back to the flat for a wash and change before going across town to the party. The December sky had just begun to unleash a penetrating drizzle when I reached into my pocket for my keys. At that precise moment, in a vision of blinding clarity, I remembered that they were on the mantelpiece of my third-floor flat. There was no point in ringing the bell. I was, in a manner of speaking, the sole resident.

I took my problem around the corner to the police station. The desk sergeant viewed me with suspicion as I babbled out my predicament. Two bored-looking policemen stood smoking by the fire and eyeing me with mild curiosity.

'We have no powers of breaking and entering,' he told me severely. 'Have you any proof that you live in this house?'

I had not a single shred of documentary evidence on my person. The sergeant studied me intently. I shuffled uncomfortably, suddenly aware that things are never as simple as they seem, not as far as policemen are concerned. The stalemate ended when the younger of the two policemen left the fire and took a hand in the affair.

'Tell you what, Sam,' he said to the sergeant, 'I'll go up with this chap and give him a leg-up over the back wall. If he can get in and show me some proof that he lives there, wouldn't that do the job?'

Sergeant Sam thought this over. 'All right,' he said, at length, 'but remember,' he cautioned me, 'this is entirely unofficial.'

The policeman and I trudged up the back entry chatting of this and that and he gave me the promised leg-up over the back wall. I dropped down on top of the bin, scattering its contents over the yard. I was still on my knees in the middle of the mess when the policeman strolled in through the entry door. It hadn't been locked.

Getting into the house was another matter entirely. There was a gap of about three inches at the top of the kitchen window, so I clambered on to the sill and managed to force it down another bit. The policeman joined me on the sill and between the two of us we cracked enough of the layers of ancient paint to release it a few inches more.

'That's your lot,' said the policeman. 'Can you get through it, do you think?'

I managed to get my head and shoulders through the opening, and the policeman had propelled me as far as my belt buckle by pushing my feet before I realised two uncomfortable things. The aerial of the landlady's electric radio also entered through the opening and was threatening to strangle me. And the sink below was brimming with water and dishes.

'How's it going?' the policeman called up from the yard.

'I'm choking,' I gasped.

'What's that you say?'

'I'm choking,' I yodelled.

He uttered an unofficial expression and vaulted nimbly up on the window sill again. The aerial was tight across my Adam's apple and the radio, on its shelf beside the window, was edging towards an expensive fall. Some unceremonious manipulation of my head freed me from strangulation. Thus liberated, I grabbed the edge of the sink and he decanted me forward in a species of forward roll into the kitchen. My descending heels caught the extended leaf of the table and brought it crashing to the floor.

'It's a good job,' the policeman remarked from his perch on the window sill,' that those dishes weren't still on the table.'

I gathered myself up off the floor and let him in. He gave me a hand to right the table and I offered to go up to the flat and get my driver's licence, for in those pre-test days, the halt, the lame and even the blind had them.

'Don't bother,' he said. 'Anybody who goes through all this rigmarole just has to be an honest man.'

With mutual wishes of all the best and similar remarks we parted company and I headed off up the stairs towards my long-delayed wash and change of clothes. As I turned on to the second-floor landing a face looked over the banister and shortened my life, of that I'm sure. Then the light snapped on. The owner of the face was Anne, from the flat next to mine. She was a very pretty, whizz-kid design student at the Art College, with a face normally composed entirely of big brown eyes and a charming smile. The smile, at that moment, was missing. In its place was a look of grim determination and she had a substantial-looking poker in one hand.

Of course, like the rest of the neighbouring male student population, I fancied her considerably, though as far as she was concerned, I was a non-person. I had the feeling that then wasn't the moment to try to improve the image. With a growing crick in my neck, for she didn't budge from her commanding position on the landing, I hastily sketched in the situation, reassuring her that the racket she heard was only myself and the forces of law and order making our entry. She listened frostily and then flounced into her flat without offering any explanation as to why she was there when every other weekend she was far away. It must be difficult to flounce if you're only five foot and a bit and wearing jeans, but she managed it. Admirably.

I never saw her again. I left the flat at the end of that term, then only a week away, because I had got tired of taking long walks or loafing on the stairs while Frank entertained one or other of his numerous girl friends. Years were to pass before the rest of the story came to light. I called into my insurance brokers one day and recognised one of the secretaries beavering away in the outer office as someone who used to frequent the student dances all those ages ago. We had the usual fancy-seeing-you-here-isn't-the-mortgage-rate-dreadful sort of exchange.

'Do you ever see Anne these days?' she asked. 'I see her quite often. Her kids and mine go to the same school. In fact I saw her last week at a parents' night and funny enough, we were talking about you.'

She leaned on her typewriter and looked earnestly at me. 'Do you know,' she said confidentially, 'she told me that she deliberately stayed over one weekend because the landlady told her you were staying over to go to a party and she was sure you'd ask her to go with you. But you never did.'

Time stood still for a moment, then shot into reverse. I pulled in the waistline and preened a bit. If youth but knew, if age but could . . . I had sized the whole situation up wrongly that night and I felt a tinge of regret.

'You missed your chance,' the secretary said lightly, as I turned to go with man-of-the-world nonchalance. 'Well, cheerio, Frank.'

Frank! Wrong again, I thought, as the landlady's voice came echoing down the years. In spite of my denying that I was Frank, she had absent-mindedly confused us again when Anne came to pay her rent. Isn't it just as well, I reflected, that there's no Santa Claus. The dozy old buffer would probably come down the wrong chimney anyway.

15 *Whaddya Think This Is, a Holiday Camp?*

If someone was to shake me awake in the middle of the night and demand to know my instant recollection of Butlins, I could reply without even opening my eyes. I can see, as clearly as in a colour photograph, a spotty, gangly, bespectacled youth coming out of a camp dance hall with his arm protectively round a very attractive girl. Tucked under his other arm, still in their cellophane wrapper, was a pair of cream-and-brown pyjamas.

'There's confidence for you,' said John Dai Hughes to me. 'Can't you just see him, standing in her chalet and taking all the pins out of those pyjamas? Bet you he puts the cardboard back inside the wrapper with the pins stuck in it, all tidy-like, and folds it up before he puts it in the little bin.'

'A fellow going to a dance with his pyjamas under his arm is capable of anything,' I replied.

This memorable event took place in the summer holidays of my first year in college and I had been engaged at enormous cost – well, eight pounds a week, plus food and accommodation – by Billy Butlin to keep order in his camp at Pwllheli. It's not easy to say, Pwllheli, but I got coaching from a friendly native. If you say 'och,' as in 'och, aye,' put a P in front and tag Lelly on behind that, you can get pretty close to it. Not close enough to fool a Welshman but enough to make me feel linguistically superior to the vast majority of the campers, who were English. They just couldn't manage that 'och' sound. Powelly and Peelyweely were the best some could manage, and local Welsh people would even accept Pithelly with a tolerant, if slightly pained, expression.

Pwllheli was definitely a camp. Every time I see a black-and-white film on television, featuring army recruits arriving at their first camp, I am instantly transported back to Pwllheli. It had a security barrier across the entrance and a guardroom – yes, that's what it was called – to one side. As each busload of new staff arrived. Sergeant Pugh emerged from his office and stood, hands on hips, looking them over. He was always on the lookout for recruits for his security staff. He was one of those men just born to wear a uniform. Ex-service, naturally, tall, thin as a whippet, knife-edge creases in the trousers ending on sparkling toecaps, sleeves neatly rolled up the sinewy, tanned arms and the sun sparkling on the gold chevrons.

'What have you come to do?' he demanded, creaking towards me in his gleaming shoes.

'Kitchen porter,' I told him, half-expecting him to bark 'Sergeant!' at me.

'Oh, you don't want to go there,' he said. 'Horrible place, the kitchens. Full of steam and heat and the smell of vegetables cooking. Have you ever smelt vegetables cooking for 2,000 people?'

'Cabbage too?' I enquired.

'You don't like cabbage?' he asked sympathetically.

'Hate the stuff,' I said.

'They cook cabbage by the ton,' he said. 'Now I've got a job for you here. Out in the open, fresh air, nice uniform. Well set up lad like you, smart uniform, the girls will love it.'

Well, I wasn't in the job many hours before I found out why the 14-man security department was always under strength. The rank-and-file deserted in a steady stream, that's why. The attractions of enforcing a one-way traffic system, clearing the pubs at closing time, breaking up fights, acting as dance-hall bouncer, getting beaten up and thrown in the pool, tended to pall in a remarkably short time.

The chief security officer was a youngish ex-army captain who prowled the camp at night wearing one of those white rubber military raincoats that flooded the market in the years after World War Two. He was a perfectly agreeable man, completely unexcitable and he conducted my training course. It lasted nearly five minutes and consisted mostly of the advice not to hit anybody first.

'Let the other fellow hit you first,' he advised. 'Then lure him back towards the guardroom. Once we get him, or them inside, we'll sort them out.'

Practical stuff, this, the kind of advice that made me wish I'd opted for the kitchens and the cabbages. As it turned out, I never needed to apply it. Eight pounds a week and a slightly comic opera-ish uniform wasn't sufficient inducement for me to risk life and limb. I made a mental note to use the softly-softly approach.

Sergeant Edgar Pugh was the second-in-command. He patrolled the camp constantly on a red bike, checking that his men were doing their stuff and radiating that air of authority that's like a second skin to senior NCOs. Next in the command structure came two corporals. One of them, a Liverpudlian called Kennedy, farmed in the area and was in charge of the night shift. The other, a Mayoman called Reilly, had taken a drop in rank and pay from the security staff of a Midlands car factory to be Sergeant Pugh's deputy in Pwllheli. Reilly tucked his trousers in the top of motorcycle boots and kept a flattened Woodbine packet wedged down the inside of his cap behind the peak. This brought the peak down over his eyes so that he walked with his head thrown back. In this get-up he was the spitting image of Goering.

I don't recall Corporal Reilly ever being around when he was needed, though I could have guessed with reasonable accuracy where he was. The purpose of his voluntary demotion and move from the car company staff was that Pwllheli, unlike the factory, bristled with women in exuberant holiday mood. He simply moved in with a different one each week. Having made his selection – and his fascist appearance, to my amazement, spoiled him for choice – he was rarely seen afterwards, except at meal-times in the staff canteen. And here another of his aberrations was evident. I would never have thought it possible that anyone could consume so much ketchup.

'I like a bit of dinner with my sauce,' he used to say. 'Keeps my strength up.' The theory may be true. I never had the chance to put it to the test. My lack of motorcycle boots probably had something to do with it. I recall that canteen with a shudder. It served us three meals a day to supplement our derisory wage and all three were identical. It's the only eating place where I've been served potatoes for breakfast. They were poured out of a jug – I wouldn't lie about this affront to our national vegetable – and they were the consistency of skimmed milk. At lunch and dinner they were slightly thicker in texture but this was mostly an illusion created by the presence of lumps of unidentifiable substances.

Every meal ended with ice-cream. It came in little cylindrical wrapped chunks and, in contrast to the potatoes, it was as solid as concrete. Alone in the middle of a soup plate, it looked like a night-light and it was proof against all cutting edges. It was impossible to anchor, and I have no recollection of its taste. Meal-breaks weren't long enough to wait for it to thaw.

The camp, like ancient Gaul, was divided into three parts, excluding the staff chalets. One was reserved for families, one for single men and one for unattached females. One of the theoretical functions of the commissionaires – us, the security staff – was to ensure that after the pubs shut and the dances were over, the single folk went home to their separate and chaste beds.

Old King Canute did a better job with the waves. Billy Butlin's moral code was unenforceable and nobody bothered too much about it. Occasionally head office got a complaint about carry-ons in the singles' chalets, and then an edict came down from on high, ordering the security staff to do their stuff. We had no incentive to do our stuff, and so the ex-army captain would appear from nowhere to stiffen our resolve. He stood at the end of a row of chalets and ordered us to knock on selected doors to discover if there were any girls in the men's chalets or men in the girls' chalets, depending on where the raid was taking place.

It was all a bit hilarious. John Dai Hughes, with whom I was paired, always knocked quietly and asked 'Have you got any women in there, boyo?' Sometimes a girl's voice would reply 'No,' from a man's chalet, whereupon John Dai would offer some advice of an improper and specific nature and we would inform the captain that all was quiet on that particular front.

We assumed that the captain couldn't possibly overhear everything that was said. We found out our mistake one night in the men's section, when he indicated a particular chalet and John Dai knocked on the door and put his question.

'Sure,' said a man's voice, 'I've got half a dozen in here. What of it?'

'Greedy bugger,' John Dai whispered back. 'Send us out a couple. Owen and I are bloody freezing out here.'

I turned round to call to the captain that strictly monastic conditions prevailed in the chalet under scrutiny. However, he had moved from his spot at the end of the row and I had actually delivered my report to the tip of his nose. He said nothing. He merely walked between the two of us and knocked on the door in an official manner. This prompted a suggestion from inside that he should go to hell and refrain from interfering in the simple pleasures of the poor holidaymakers. A chorus of giggling accompanied this advice.

A second bout of authoritative knocking put a stop to that, and the door opened reluctantly, to reveal that the man hadn't been boasting. There were six girls in the chalet, though to be fair, there were also six men. Twelve people in a space meant to accommodate only three was serious overcrowding, which is one possible, though improbable, explanation for the fact that they were all stark naked.

The captain stepped into the middle of them, in his white rubber coat, and read them a riot act that would have done credit to a bishop. From our place on the veranda, John Dai and I heard every carefully selected, skin-stripping word, delivered in a normal conversational tone.

'Strict chapel, him,' John Dai whispered to me. 'We're for the chop tomorrow, you'll see.'

The captain came out, closed the door and stood looking at his watch. It seemed like hours, but it could only have been minutes, before the door opened and six silent girls, more or less dressed, filed out past him. Then he swished away in his rubber coat. In spite of John Dai's gloomy forecast, we heard nothing more about the incident and our dereliction of duty. There turned out to be a simple explanation. The season was by then more than half over and the supply of recruits had dwindled to nothing. We were better than nothing but only just.

Occasionally adventure was thrust upon me in my capacity as security man. One night after closing time, a man armed with a knife chose to barricade himself in an office. I don't know why he did this and I have no feelings of gratitude, even after all this time, towards the camper who drew this development to my attention.

I went along to the office and invited him to come out. This was stalling tactics. I had no desire whatever to come to close quarters with him. He brandished his knife through the broken glass panel and offered to disembowel me and several other commissionaires who had joined me by this stage. We collectively declined his offer. None of us was of the stuff that heroes are made from. We conferred among ourselves about what to do, surrounded by a crowd avid for action, preferably bloodstained, so long as it wasn't their blood. In the midst of our deliberations, the man flung open the door, charged through our terrified ranks and fled into a nearby kitchen.

We commissionaires followed at a more sedate pace and found him just inside the door, with his back to a line of women washing dishes. He continued to flourish the knife and repeat his offer. He was certainly newfangled with the word 'disembowel.' One of the women turned round, flicked her drying cloth under her arm in a practised movement, twisted his arm up his back and tossed the knife into a sinkful of suds, as if disarming deranged youths was simply part of her job description. She wasn't much over five foot and pushing pension age. Her name was Aggie, and every year she made the journey from Belfast's Newtownards Road to Wales to wash dishes in one of Billy Butlin's kitchens. She was a better security man than all of us put together.

One of my duties was to operate the barrier at the main entrance, and Sergeant Pugh was certainly right about the open-air value of the job. When it rained, which it often did, I got soaked. The uniform issue included a greatcoat completely useless for anything short of a blizzard and a plastic raincoat that was worse than a Turkish bath on a wet August day. When the weather was good, and sometimes it was, eight hours of lounging against the barrier turned me lobster colour. It was this ruddy, outdoor appearance that led me to a brief and profitable sideline.

One fine day I was approached by two stout ladies and a pair of gentlemen also built on generous lines. They had rugs and picnic baskets, and the stouter of the two ladies eyed me before venturing the opinion that I was a likely-looking lad. This is an expression capable of a variety of interpretations, not all favourable,

but in this case flattering. From my sunburnt complexion she had assumed that I was a son of the local soil and therefore well versed in the signs and portents of weather forecasting.

'Will it rain today?' she asked.

'Definitely not,' I said, with the unshakeable confidence of the totally ignorant.

Well, naturally, she wanted to know how I knew. It was easy enough. It hadn't rained for almost a week, the sky was a brilliant blue but I couldn't tell them that and shatter my new-found image as an oracle. I looked about me for inspiration and noticed a faint haze on the top of a not-too-distant mountain. Its outline was similar to Crockmore, a mountain that broods over my own Drumderg. Local wisdom there was that a faint haze on its top meant a fine day and if you couldn't see it at all the rain was already bucketing down.

I drew their attention to the haze and hinted that my secret lay in interpreting the density of it. They went on their way well satisfied. I was still at my post when they came back several hours later, and the spokeswoman pressed a half-crown into my underpaid palm.

Every day that week they sought me out and I pontificated to the value of a half-crown before they set off for their picnic. They too seemed to have no love for the liquid potatoes, for they never ate in the camp, and it was a boast of the catering department that the staff and campers got exactly the same menus. They went home on the Saturday and before they left, the leader of the quartet presented me with an autograph book and asked for my name and address. She intended writing to me for a made-to-measure forecast before her next year's holidays. She also slipped a 10-bob note into my shirt pocket. I didn't get a request for a forecast the following year, but somebody else might have. You see, I gave the name and address of a fellow-student in Newtownards.

My stint at Butlins was my first employment outside Ireland and it opened my eyes to many things, not the least the question of nationality. It was the first time I heard the theory that St Patrick was a Welshman. Ron Richards made this allegation one day as we were sweeping out the guardroom, and as proof of his conviction he offered to fight me.

If I should win, I put it to Ron, would the saint then automatically become Irish? He would not, Ron assured me, because right was might in this instance, so there was no question of my winning. He adopted a Marquis of Queensberry pose and shadow boxed a bit in a very professional sort of way. If I were to introduce the shovel I was holding into the contest, thus ensuring victory, would the Irish patron saint cease to be Welsh?

Ron said that wouldn't be fighting fair. I told him that where I came from, spades and scythes were often introduced into brawls. I quoted several examples of this from the local petty sessions. At this point Ron said the thing wasn't worth arguing over and instead brought me up to date on his love-life, which was complicated to an unbelievable extent. How he ever found time to formulate theories about St Patrick is beyond me.

Like Corporal Reilly, Ron had given up a job in his home town in South Wales to work in the camp as a commissionaire. He had left a regular girlfriend behind, too, and he had another one installed in his chalet. That was only the start of it. No matter who had the duty of watching over Reception on Saturdays, Ron always swopped with him when the new campers came in. Those of us who were off-duty used to ramble round to Reception on Saturdays to watch Ron sizing up the incoming talent. You can see the same look on a farmer's face round the parade ring at any agricultural show.

Some of the best crack in the camp was watching Ron in action during the week. He had the standard 40 hours to punch in, and all the overtime he could get to beef up the basic eight pounds. He had to write a daily letter to the girlfriend at home, read the one that arrived daily for him, and keep all this secret from the girl in his chalet. In addition, he generally culled out one, and if possible two, nubile young women from each Saturday's intake. And he had to keep his total camp harem in ignorance of the others. You could get breathless just watching him.

He was invariably broke. One by one he sold off his personal possessions to finance his hectic lifestyle, until he had only one item left. It was his Rolls razor and one day, in the canteen, somewhere between the liquid potatoes and the rock-hard ice-cream, he offered it to me for two pounds.

A Rolls razor came in a kind of kit. The lid of the stainless steel box contained a whetstone and the bottom held a strop. You took the bottom off the box, fitted the handle and trundled the head back and forth in its grooves over the whetstone. When you put the bottom back on and removed the top, you were stropping the edge, or putting the finishing touches to it. It was a wickedly sharp gadget and had an ingeniously mounted guard to prevent the user from digging blood-stained lumps out of himself. I haggled, for it was what they call in marketing circles a distress sale, and eventually I got it for 30 bob.

Now Ron had pimples and whatever the source of his skin problem, I didn't want any of it, so I took the razor to the camp hospital and discussed the problem in a roundabout sort of a way with the nurse. She snapped her fingers.

'Why don't I sterilise it in the autoclave?' she suggested.

'Now there's a brilliant idea,' I said, so we had a cup of coffee while the actoclave worked its magic and we talked of many things. When she fished the razor out it was germ-free. And useless. The intense heat of the autoclave had left the strop looking like a bit of hosepipe. The experience wasn't a complete loss, though. It was the beginning of a cosy friendship with the nurse.

It wasn't always possible to give Reception duty to Ron, and one Saturday I was there, resplendent in white shirt, blue-and-cream tie, blue peaked cap and blue trousers with a gold stripe down the leg. It was my duty to give directions and look useful. When I heard a voice shouting 'Paddy!' I paid no attention. When the voice snarled, 'You deaf, Paddy?' right at my elbow, I turned and look down at the bald pate of a brick-coloured specimen in knee-length, Desert Army surplus shorts, open sandals and ankle socks. The sun had never set on his empire and every man could whip his own houseboys.

'See those bags?' he snapped, all business, 'Carry them to my chalet.'

'Carry them yourself,' I told him, Bogart-style, out of the side of my mouth. This disconcerted him.

'I'll report you,' he said, a little less confident.

'You do that, friend,' I advised, borrowing the line from John Wayne.

'Sorry, mate,' he said, contritely, 'I didn't know you were a Geordie.' And he tottered off lugging his own luggage.

When my weather forecasting sideline dried up, I found a better one with the Liverpudlian night corporal, Kennedy, who farmed nearby. He paid me the standard camp rate to help out on his farm on my days off. That too came to an unexpected end during the haymaking season.

'I suppose you won't be able to come tomorrow,' he said to me one day. 'You'll want to go off boozing with your friends from Ireland.'

'Why should I want to do that?' I asked.

'Big day in Ireland,' said Kennedy, 'Orangemen's Day.'

'Goodness gracious me,' I said, or words to that effect, 'You're mistaken. I will not be wanting the day off.'

'Oh,' he said sourly, 'You're one of the other crowd are you?'

I got no more haymaking overtime from him but I wasn't all that bothered. It was hard work – which was one of the reasons I'd left home that summer anyway. I may not have made hay while the sun shone but I came home marginally better off than I'd left. I'd carried no man's bags, either, but I'd survived. That's the greatest Irish trick of all.

16   *Valentine's Night Massacre*

My father had strong views on dancing. Like clergymen and sin, he was against it. His views weren't shared by any of his offspring, or by my aunts. They were of the opinion, not expressed in his hearing, that his dislike of dancing stemmed from his own lack of talent in that direction.

I wouldn't like to say for sure what precise characteristics I inherited from him, but I think we did have one thing in common. As far as dancing was concerned, I seemed to have more left feet than a right-footed man should have, I wasn't too good on corners and I was something of a danger in traffic. Given this disadvantage it was all the more remarkable that I should have got involved in the St Valentine's Night dance at all.

I don't remember any great fuss being made about Valentine's Day around Draperstown though I may subconsciously have blotted the whole business from my memory. Anyway, it seemed to me that it was just coincidence.

The dance that night in 1957 was in Dungiven, which is separated from Draperstown by a range of mountains, though there is ample access in the form of hilly roads. These hilly roads had much to do with the events of that night. Nine people, four couples and the driver, who had high hopes of good hunting at the dance, set out at a reasonable hour to whoop it up in Dungiven.

The car was John's pride and joy. It was his first car, and as everyone knows, there is no car like your first one. There was certainly no car like this one. It was basically an Austin but down the years so many bits had fallen off and not been replaced or replaced with bits from other cars, that it was no longer identifiable as any particular model. John was a born tinkerer and he had a theory that petrol engines could be made to run on tractor fuel, provided the right modifications were made to the engine. He had actually carried out some modifications but they didn't prevent the car from being very sick a lot of the time. It was also, as he put it himself, using a wee sup of oil, so between the grey smoke produced by the tractor fuel and the stink of burning oil, the overall effect was of a particularly asthmatic Chitty Chitty Bang Bang on a very bad day.

Then there were the girls. The dirndl skirt came into its own that year, so that a couple of girls dressed for a dance filled the average car. Getting four such girls and their partners into one car called for methods that are only employed on Japanese underground stations these days. The fellows got in first, the girls arranged themselves on their laps, and we set off. You might image that this kind of overcrowding would have led to a certain cosiness. It led to ice in the atmosphere. The girls had spent hours getting ready and they were going to emerge from this car looking as if they had been dragged backwards through a hedge. I had Kate on my lap and I envied John. As the driver, he had a seat all to himself.

Not that there would have been much to complain about in having Kate parked on my lap in ordinary circumstances. She was blonde, blue eyed and had the kind of shape that made toothless old men manage to dredge up a whistle. She was also acknowledged to be a brilliant dancer, so what she was doing in my company requires some explanation. She was a visitor to the neighbourhood and her aunt had apparently drawn up a list of young men in whose company it was respectable to be seen. I wasn't on it. Kate was sharing this journey into the unknown with me simply because she was, as they used to say in those parts, a contrary article. The best way to get her to do something was to forbid it.

There were several technical problems to be overcome. Due to certain deficiencies in the lights, John drove with his head out of the window. Then there was the gear-stick. It was buried under mounds of dirndl skirt and for reasons of delicacy could only be operated by the wearer. When gear changes were necessary John would shout 'Now' and she would rummage frantically among the layers of skirt and shove the lever in the direction he called out. Sometimes it worked. Mostly it didn't and the car came to a wheezing halt.

There was a hill a mile long to be negotiated. The car refused to have anything to do with it. Two by two the couples got out but it still behaved like a horse shying away from a jump. Even when John had the vehicle to himself, it would only co-operate when he turned it round and reversed it up the slope.

We walked behind in two groups, four girls, four men, in a silence that lasted halfway up the hill. That's when we got the first puncture. This roadside repair took all four of us men, working under John's direction, for all the jack points were rotten. The only way we could prop the car up was on stones, every one of which had to be prised from a nearby ditch. We had no tools for loosening stones and we weren't dressed for carrying them either, so by the time the job was finished no respectable hall would have let us in without demanding some guarantee of good behaviour. We certainly wouldn't have got any character references from the girls, standing in a silent, teeth-chattering group on a mountain road 1,500 feet above sea-level.

We resumed our funereal progress for all of another 200 yards. That's when the second tyre burst. John was, however, a man of prudence, and kept a supply of odd wheels in the boot as a precaution against multiple punctures. So we did it all again, in a hostile atmosphere that wasn't at all helped by John's remark that we would probably get in free because it was after 12.

In fact the car park was empty and the band were loading up their instruments when we arrived. We decided that having come so far we might as well go in anyway, just to have it to say that we had completed the journey under the most adverse of circumstances. The caretaker was brushing the floor and he surveyed us with a sardonic eye as we trudged in. He showed the girls to seats and brought them soft drinks, which they consumed wordlessly. He surveyed the evidence of the roadside repairs on our crumpled suits then he produced a couple of extra brushes and a shovel.

'Give me a bit of a hand,' he said. 'You're dressed for it.'

We got home silently and uneventfully, for it was downhill all the way. By the time I got in it was after six and I had a premonition of trouble brewing. Midnight, or maybe one in the morning, my father might tolerate. Six was confrontation time.

The grandfather clock that stood on our landing for generations hadn't struck the hour in living memory. This was due to a defect in the weights engineered by a latecoming member of the previous generation anxious to avoid the wrath of my grandfather. It still ticked remorselessly away, and my father maintained that when it reached the hour, it emitted a particularly loud tick of what I suppose was reproach at the vandalism to its innards. This tick, although I could never identify it as different from any other, was sufficient to waken my father. From inside his closed room he would inform the latecomer that it was one o'clock in the morning, or whatever. He was always right too. The announcement of the time was usually a prelude to a lengthy lecture on the culprit's shortcomings.

I stopped at the milk-house just inside the yard gate, removed my shoes and tiptoed across the yard and into the house. This part was easy, for the front door was never locked. I crept into the kitchen and sat in the armchair by the fire to consider the next move. Our stairs had only one creaky board but it was on a different step each night I came home late. My feet were freezing from the jaunt across the frosty yard, so I rested them on the edge of the range while I gave my earnest consideration to the hurdles and hazards of getting up to my room without the traditional sermon reserved for these occasions.

I closed my eyes, all the better to concentrate and before I knew it, the kitchen was ablaze with light and somebody was vigorously shaking my shoulder. It was my father, fully dressed.

'You're up early this morning,' he said sarcastically and stalked out to begin the morning's milking. It was a watershed in our relationship. One by one the older members of the family had been reprimanded for their late hours and one by one he had given up on them. Then it was my turn. I was 20 years old after all and living most of my time in the sinful city, where maybe I never went to bed at all.

John's modified motor also surrendered to the inevitable two days later. He was driving past the parochial house when it emitted its final asthmatic wheeze, and its last cloud of grey smoke, and died in the street without benefit of clergy.

Kate emigrated to Canada soon afterwards. Some years later her aunt spoke to me for the first time on the subject of the Valentine's Night fiasco. Kate, she told me, had married a rich Canadian and lived a life of luxury. It was her due, she managed to imply, as she sketched in the details of her niece's prosperous lifestyle. Every year her doting husband presented her with a brand new Pontiac. Automatic, of course. The aunt was attaching far more significance to that St Valentine's Night than it deserved. I didn't like to tell her she was rubbing salt into wounds that didn't exist. It would have come across as sour grapes.

17 Throwing the Bucket

I spent the summer of 1958 driving a dumper on a building site in Cumberland. The place was called Spadeadam, and about 2,000 of us were building a rocket station about the size of an Irish townland, or maybe two.

By the time I arrived on the site the project was 24 million pounds over budget and only one tiny building was operational. There was no proper access to it and the scientists had to scramble over piles of rubble to get in and out. This did their white wellington boots no good at all.

There were two main reasons for the delay. One was an obstreperous local farmer whose farm was right in the middle of the site. He refused point-blank to leave and it's fair to say that his thrawn attitude towards the enforced purchase of his land afforded much joy to the Irish on the site. And the work-force was mostly Irish. The other reason was that one of the subcontractors was on strike the whole summer. Each morning his electricians queued up before their site office and did nothing. It was all a bit silly, for the work went on round them.

The bricklayers were on piece-work and they worked their hodsmen like galley-slaves. Or they would have, except for Ginger. Ginger operated a cement mixer on the section I was working on and he was one of the more elegant workers on the site. He wore a double-breasted suit and never even took his tie off even on the hottest day. He arrived late every morning and the only preparation he made for the day's labours was to tuck the bottoms of his trousers into his socks. At ten he went off for his tea-break. The time allowed was 15 minutes but Ginger rarely came back much before 11 o'clock. By this time the bricklayers had run out of mortar and were looking for blood. But Ginger was impervious to abuse and threats and when, inevitably, he was sacked he took no notice of that either. In fact a bout of fisticuffs between him and the new appointee took place before he conceded defeat and stalked off, his tea mug an unsightly bulge in his jacket pocket.

If Ginger was idle, the new man brought incompetence to new depths. He hadn't mastered the art and inner mystery of mixing mortar in the right proportions. The bricklayers could at least build with Ginger's product, but the replacement's was little

more than greenish liquid. I knew he was destined for the chop
the first time I nosed the dumper under the mixer platform and
saw the stuff cascading down. He was barely half a day in the job
before a delegation of wrathful bricklayers shinned down the
scaffolding and waited on the general foreman, demanding his
head. I was actually driving up to the platform when he took his
leave. And he made a dramatic exit. As I approached from one
direction, a party of visiting dignitaries led by the site agent was
coming from the other and I drew in to let them pass. The
dismissed mixer-operator called the site agent over.

'Yes, what is it?' the agent demanded impatiently.

'I just wanted to wish you the best of luck, sor,' said the
mixer-man, taking off his cap with his left hand and tugging his
forelock – the only time I've ever seen it done – with his right.
Then he tipped the contents of his mixer over the party, vaulted
nimbly down from his platform and stomped off. It was many
years later that I learned that 'sor' is not a corruption of 'sir' as the
stage Irish would have us think. It is, in fact, the Irish for 'louse.'

My general foreman was a Scot called Jake and he wasn't too
keen on students about the site. In fact the number of things Jake
disliked would have filled a modest-sized encyclopedia. He
tolerated me, just about, because he had formed the impression
that I was the personnel manager's nephew. I was no relation
whatever to Charlie O'Kane, the personnel manager, but I had
met him the summer before in Draperstown. His brother was
married to my cousin Rose and out of this chance encounter a
lucrative summer job emerged. Twenty-five pounds a week after
a nominal deduction for food and accommodation in the comfort-
able camp already built for the RAF was a considerable improve-
ment on the previous summer's eight pounds a week, plus the
good chance of getting beaten up. Charlie was a big, amiable
Kilrea man who, however, didn't suffer fools gladly. It was for
this quality that Jake tolerated me about his section of the site.

If I had been an art student, his attitude would have been
different. His last art student had departed for unspecified
reasons just before I arrived. Jake was an unlikely patron of the
arts, but nonetheless his personal art student had had the life of a
white dog, as the Irish proverb so quaintly puts it. If rumour, and
Jake, were to be believed, he did nothing all day but sit in Jake's
hut, decorating the foreman's lunch-box and assorted personal
possessions with drawings of naked women. Jake had a particular weakness for this art form and it accounted for his having an
artist in his entourage, in the manner of a medieval prince.

In a curious form of oneupmanship, another foreman, a born
hypochondriac, had a personal medical student. He was permitted to do nothing heavier than make the tea, which was a
full-time job in itself. Any form of labouring, in the foreman's

opinion, might damage his hands and thus endanger his future career. In the meantime he consulted the student on every ailment under the sun. This idyllic existence ended when it came to light that the student had in fact been cast out of his medical school due to a chronic inability to pass examinations. Hell hath no fury to match that of a hypochondriac foreman whose personal physician has been exposed as a quack.

Most of the Irish on the site were working all the hours God sent to get together the price of a farm or business back home but I came on one man who had taken a different line. I met him in a site hut when we were sheltering from a downpour. He was working with an assortment of plumbing that looked like the makings of a giant hypodermic. It turned out that he was a soil tester by profession. His job was to draw up samples of soil from various levels and advise on the viability of laying a pipeline or building a road over the spot.

'How did you get to be a soil tester?' I asked.

'I'm well qualified,' he said. 'I was a farmer. I own nearly a hundred acres in Tipperary.'

I expressed the view that he was moving against the trend.

'Listen,' he said. 'I had a couple of nephews working for me, the biggest pair of rascals unhung. If I could have bored into them with that contraption,' he prodded the testing equipment with his boot, 'I'd have found no work in them. All they wanted to do was smoke, drink and play cards. And they were always after me to see which of them I'd leave the place to. Leave the place to! I was only 35 at the time and still thinking of getting married. The pair of whelps were only about 20 and they were trying to tell me I had one foot in the grave.'

'So what happened?'

'Oh, I just cleared out,' he told me. 'In 1932.'

'But that was 26 years ago,' I said. 'Do you go back often?'

'I headed off once,' he said. 'I came down from Scotland as far as Carlisle and I met a man that was going to build tank traps along the south coast. I was only going home for a while, to buy a couple of barrels of porter and throw a dance for the neighbours, maybe tell them a few lies. But there was good money at the digging, so I went down south instead.'

'What has happened to your place since then?' I said, in some disbelief.

'I don't know and I don't care,' he said. 'Maybe it's all rushes. I'm as happy as Larry. The nephews can't get it. And,' he added with a grin, 'neither can their mothers.' And he gathered up his gear and went off whistling in the rain. It seemed an extreme form of family feud, but then we Irish are bloody-minded to an astonishing degree.

Plinney was another interesting character on that site. He was more widely known as Bowler and the Plinney derived from his pronunciation of 'plenty.' Nobody knew his real name and he answered to either nickname. He had an unholy expertise with the bucket, weighing half a ton or thereabouts, that was attached to the end of the crane he operated. He had been ticked off years before by a foreman for some of his more hair-raising stunts, and his professional pride had been stung to the point where he decided to kill the foreman by unleashing his deadly bucket at his head the first chance he got.

His aim was so precise that in fact he tipped the foreman's bowler off his head without otherwise causing him the slightest damage. Humiliated by this failure to assassinate the foreman, he climbed down from the cab and followed him to the site canteen intent on finishing the job with his fists.

'I couldn't believe it,' he said to me. 'I walked into that canteen and do you know what? There he was, telling his mates all about it. He was saying, "He's some hand with the bucket, that Plinney, he actually tipped the hat right off my head and I hardly even felt it".'

In view of this tribute he cancelled his intention to kill the foreman. The nickname Bowler originated at that moment. He was quite proud of it. He was a superstitious character and believed that whistling in bed would bring untold misfortune in its wake. It was a belief of possibly Freudian origin, for it was well known that he was bigamously married to an assortment of ladies up and down the British Isles, one in proximity to each site he had worked on.

Then there was Scunner – and the name was well deserved, because he had a perpetual scowl on his face.

'Come here you,' he snarled at me one evening as I passed his table in the canteen. 'Where are you from?'

'Draperstown,' I informed him, confident that no one but myself on that moor would have heard of the place. My confidence was misplaced. He reeled off the names of all the pubs in the village with a comment on their willingness, or lack of it, to serve drink after hours. I asked him how he knew all these places but I never did find out his connection with my home town, which was infuriating for he kept dropping tantalising comments every time we met.

Our paths crossed once more. It was in Belfast, during my final year in college, and I met him walking along the Antrim Road in his socks. He was otherwise fully dressed. He ordered me round to his house for a cup of tea and let me know that in exchange for his hospitality I would be required to give my opinion of a play he had written.

The house was immaculate. Cosy even to the extent of a cat sleeping on her back on the hearthrug. He explained that she was a stray that had adopted him but she had been struck down by some mysterious feline illness soon after her arrival. She had responded to whiskey administered with an eye-dropper. In fact she had developed quite a fondness for the prescription and she was, even as we spoke, sleeping off a hangover. That, at least, was his explanation for her unusual sleeping posture.

Scunner's version of tea-making consisted of emptying most of a packet of tea into two mugs and adding hot water and five spoonfuls of sugar. The real test of tea, he said, was to stick a spoon upright in it and see if it keeled over gently.

I couldn't make head or tail of the play, for the pages weren't numbered, some had been savaged by the cat and he kept producing others from under cushions or out of his pockets. I assured him that the opus was great stuff, whereupon he revealed that he had been merely canvassing a second opinion. He had already consulted J. J. Campbell, a senior lecturer in Trench House where I was a student. J. J. was a man with a gift for putting people in their places, and I tried to visualise the look on his face when the dreaded Scunner appeared before him clutching his literary offspring and demanding an audience.

'What did Mr Campbell say about it?' I asked.

'He told me,' said Scunner gravely, 'that he wasn't qualified to criticise the work of a genius.'

My dumper-driving ended the day the drive shaft broke, a happening which Vic, the transport manager, took to heart. 'We don't have an endless supply of dumpers, you know,' he told me coldly and I found myself demoted to wheelbarrow driver.

Not a very demanding job, you might think, but this was wheelbarrow-driving with a difference. I was stationed on the scaffolding and another wheelbarrow operative placed the full barrow of mortar on a little platform at ground level. My job was to haul this platform up, by means of a block-and-tackle mechanism, to where the bricklayers were working. This was deemed to be more efficient than using hodsmen. I soon changed all that. The bricklayers worked in a blur of arms and trowels and their appetite for mortar was insatiable. When I had hauled the barrow up I had to race it along the catwalk and deposit equal amounts of mortar on each mortar board, then race back, lower the wheelbarrow, wait for it to be filled, haul it back up, race back along the catwalk and repeat the process, again and again and again . . .

Sounds simple. Energetic but simple. In fact it was a minefield of hazards. For a start, it was difficult to measure out three or four equal parts of mortar simply by tilting the barrow. And they had to be equal. If they weren't it meant that one or other of the bricklayers had to wait for fresh supplies while his mates, who'd got more, were beavering away. The one who got short measure didn't like it. Lost time was lost money and it seemed I always short-changed the same man. He didn't smoke, while the others did, so he couldn't even have a quick drag while he waited.

He was reputed to be a good-living, God-fearing class of a fellow, but I took leave to doubt that, for he had a store of cusswords that could have cleaned rust off the scaffolding. It wasn't simply a case of equal shares anyway, for the barrow, like every wheelbarrow in the company's fleet, had the inevitable wobbly wheel. It pulled to the left, or open, side of the catwalk. There was a safety rail, of course, at exactly the right height to rip the skin off all my left knuckles as I fought to keep the mad machine on the straight and narrow.

Inanimate objects, I firmly believe, have a mind of their own. When I was trundling the empty barrow back it would inexplicably pull to the right. One way or another it seemed determined to pull me over the side and leave me without a functioning knuckle on either hand. Occasionally, for variety, the wheel would jam between the planks, or the whole barrow would wedge itself between the edge of the catwalk and the safety rail. This meant that some of the load was spilled, sometimes to the detriment of people below, for there were only two safety helmets on the site, Visiting Important Persons for the use of.

Finally one day, maddened by the heat, the bleeding knuckles and the colourful vocabulary of the good-living bricklayer, I let the eccentric machine have its way and plunge over the side. I watched it with grim satisfaction as it buried itself in a huge pile of sand several storeys below. I followed it down in more leisurely and orthodox fashion to where I met Jake.

'Where are you off to?' he asked.

'Draperstown,' I told him tersely.

'Never heard of it,' he answered, without a trace of regret at my departure.

Somebody at the site office must have heard of it, though, for the day after I got home a registered letter arrived from the company. It contained all the money due to me. There was no hint of reproach at the abrupt leaving. And no mention of the wheelbarrow either.

18 *No Time to Talk, William*

Shopping isn't my favourite activity. I make a couple of commando-style raids into town every year, armed with a list and a burning desire to clip a couple of minutes off my previous personal best time. There are times, however, when I am obliged, never mind by whom, to be a sort of one-man bearer-cum-retinue around the shops and I spend my waiting time loafing against some appropriate structure and watching the world go by.

During one of these expeditions I spotted another man leaning against another pillar and staring into space. There was something familiar about him but I was beset by doubts as well. It took a great leap of the imagination to turn the scruffy and rebellious youth I knew in St Columb's into the respectable, middle-aged, middle-class citizen I saw before me.

As I watched, I saw him stiffen and sort of come to attention, like an indifferent soldier who sees the sergeant-major bearing down on him. Only this sergeant-major was a decidedly presentable lady carrying a number of garments over her arm. She presented each in turn. He said something and stifled a yawn. She was not pleased with his lack of enthusiasm. Storm clouds formed overhead. She whirled and went away. He thrust his hands into his pockets and walked carefully down the aisle between the counters, methodically placing one foot before the other on the line between the tiles.

It was Billy. No doubt about it. The last time I saw those splay feet walking a line, the line was the top of the corrugated-iron fence on the top of a cliff overlooking the Brandywell. It marked the boundary of the St Columb's grounds and provided a handy vantage point for watching a Saturday afternoon match. I have no idea how high that cliff was, but when the goalkeeper kicked the ball away, it was at the height of its parabola before the sound reached us.

I'll never forget the first time I saw Billy spring on top of that wobbly fence and walk the length of it. Nobody in his right mind would have leaned on it, let along walk on it, but then the subject of Billy's mind was one that exercised the entire school staff. They were fairly evenly divided into two camps. One held that the space between his ears was empty and the other argued that it was solid bone.

'Get down,' we yelled as one man, 'you'll fall!'

Billy ignored us and continued his journey as far as the strainer post, hands and feet at right angles to the rest of his body, and tongue pointing forward. At the strainer post he turned and travelled back nonchalantly. He actually ran the last few feet and dropped lightly to the ground.

'Falling's nothing,' he assured us, 'it's the sudden stop that hurts you.'

He had sauntered off, hands in pockets and feet still at more or less the same angle that had kept him safe on the fence. It was just another incident that added to his already considerable reputation for lunatic behaviour.

And now he turned in his Walter Mitty tightrope-walking and caught my eye. He hesitated for a second or two, recognition dawned, and he came towards me with outstretched hand. We exchanged career notes. It turned out he was something impressive in the head office of a bank. I was only mildly surprised to find that old bolshie Billy had joined the capitalist classes. Teenage rebels invariably do, once the hair starts to thin and the waist begins to thicken.

We reflected for some time on the iniquities of our school life. I reminded Billy of the time a party of us had been sent, in the interests of our cultural development, to see a performance of *Twelfth Night* in Magee College.

We were in the nominal charge of a young newly appointed lay member of staff who, at an early stage in the evening, developed an amiable relationship with his opposite number from one of the city's girls' schools. At the end of the play the young teacher, having other fish to fry, dispatched us back to school under Billy's command. It may have seemed like a good idea, for Billy was a senior pupil. It was in fact a cardinal error of judgement for which I'm sure he paid dearly in the privacy of the principal's office.

We set off for the school. It's not a huge distance from Magee College to Bishop Street, so Billy decided that new and uncharted ways had to be found. He led us in all directions, walking in the middle of the road, reciting *The Pied Piper of Hamelin*. He knew only a line here and there but his decidedly blue improvisations were an entertaining substitute. Our erratic and noisy progress was inevitably reported to the school. Billy had led us through the garden of one opulent residence where he decided to demonstrate his contempt for the capitalist classes by peeing in a flower bed just inside the gate. That was after he had selected a rose to wear between his teeth and sundry other floral adornments for his hair and pockets. The teacher, I am convinced, ended up a sadder and wiser man. Billy did more to alert him to the pitfalls of his profession than any amount of training could have done.

Billy, for his part, recalled for me the Polishing Incident, as though I could ever forget it. One night just before the Hallowe'en break, it had occurred to me and a few other mischievous souls to sneak about in the dead of night and smear shoe polish on the faces of our sleeping fellows.

We were engaged in this pursuit around two in the morning when one of the victims announced loudly that he knew me. I wasn't unduly worried. It would have taken more skill than I possessed to smear shoe polish on somebody's face without waking them, but the other victims had preferred to play possum.

Next morning when the dean was supervising his flock filing into chapel he was apparently struck by the number of Kentucky minstrels he had acquired overnight. We polishers had overlooked the dubious washing habits of small boys, and while some of them appeared white enough from the front, they were black when viewed from the side. The dean was new, he was zealous and when he demanded an explanation he got one. He got it from the lad who had announced he knew me, a lad who was well connected, with parents well placed to make trouble. Names were named, for the lofty tradition of never shopping a fellow-pupil had never been very entrenched in the boarding schools of Ireland.

When the rest of the boarders departed that afternoon for the four-day break, we four polishers stayed behind. For the next two days we spent the daylight hours confined to a short stretch of unheated, terrazzo corridor, and the next two nights in our unheated rooms. By the beginning of the third day we had apparently consumed all the leftover heels of loaves in the kitchen and were permitted to depart for home. It was a kind of expulsion in reverse, but if it was meant to develop respect for the system it failed.

My father, perhaps recognising in me the qualities that had made him a thorn in the military side, said nothing when I turned up two days later than expected. Well, he did remark that he could have done with a couple of extra hands at the potato-sorting, but that was only the practical countryman in him coming to the fore.

Not all discipline in St Columb's was of the confrontational type, as Billy and I agreed. Psychology, for example, rather than blanket prohibition, led to the almost complete eradication of smoking among the pupils. Youngsters have been attracted to smoking since time immemorial, to the chagrin of their elders, who generally saw nothing contradictory in smoking incessantly while denying the same dubious privilege to their offspring. St Columb's had taken the conventional line. Smoking was a hanging offence.

The effect of this prohibition was that smoke arose from behind every tree, out of every toilet, every nook and cranny in the grounds. People living in the streets round about used to allege that a pall of cigarette smoke hung over the entire establishment night and day. Then, some time before I arrived on the scene, a new principal came up with a simple solution. He legalised smoking and changed the atmosphere forever. It wasn't a general carte blanche, far from it. First of all, it was restricted to those senior pupils who could produce a letter from their parents giving their blessing to the activity. This requirement soon fell into disuse due to large-scale forgery of these documents.

Secondly, smoking was restricted to certain times. One smoke after breakfast, another at lunch-time, one after dinner, one at the study-break at 25 past six, and the last gasp was after supper. That was about eight o'clock. The third and most important condition was that smoking should be restricted to the smoking room. If this conjures up an image of velvet smoking-jackets and Victorian elegance, forget it. The smoking room was a corrugated-iron shed, with benches round the walls, no floor and no door. It was tacked on to the side of a classroom block behind the main buildings. Its users invariably referred to it as the Reekin' Room. This was apt in several ways.

The principal let it be known that the Reekin' Room was a privilege that existed at his pleasure. One hint of misuse and it would be shut down, in so far as a building without a door could be shut down. No smoking was to take place outside its confines by anyone. There would be no appeal against his decision. The psychology was flawless. Smoking dwindled to a negligible level. The handful who used the room were recruited in one move to the side of the angels. No junior dared produce a cigarette. It was one thing to defy the authority of the staff, but to jeopardise the privileges of a senior boy was to invite retribution on a painful scale, including the confiscation of the offender's supply and its reallocation to the stock belonging to the hardened sinners.

Ten minutes was the maximum stay permitted in the Reekin' Room and punctually on the tenth minute the dean could be depended on to swoop down from his office and chase its occupants. By siting the shed as far from civilisation as possible, several of the valuable minutes could be used up just getting there. The outcome of this ingenious strategy was that by the time I left St Columb's barely a dozen people, of whom I was one but Billy wasn't, were using the shed. It fell into complete disuse soon afterwards.

This enlightened approach to a thorny problem wasn't general. The rules forbade newspapers and radios, and although cameras weren't banned specifically, their use was not encouraged. All this seems odd when you consider that the day-boys, who after all formed the majority of the enrolment, had unrestricted access to all these items. One naive parent wondered to the principal if she could give her lad a small radio for his birthday. 'Certainly not,' he said and that was the end of the matter. It may have been the end of that particular request but there were more makeshift radios in St Columb's than would have been uncovered in a sweep of a PoW camp. Most of them were made by Billy, and one of them ended up in my possession.

It worked, up to a point, through a pair of army surplus headphones with ear-pieces the size of Paris buns. An obliging day-boy brought in a coil of telephone wire to serve as an aerial. Unfortunately, the wire had been in a coil for so long that it refused to uncoil when I hung it out of the window. I thought I could remedy this by hanging a full water jug on the end but I never got to find out how effective this was. While the jug swung back and forth, the principal chose to enter the building by the side door immediately below my room, three floors down. The swaying jug, ever so gently, carried the hat off his head. He must have been preoccupied with weightier matters and assumed the wind was responsible, for he simply retrieved his hat and never looked up.

Billy was a fellow of infinite resource where dodging work was concerned and one of his chief claims to fame was the ingenious cogging machine he fabricated for his own use. Cogging was the time-honoured activity of bringing vital pieces of information into the examination room and using them to fill the gaps that ought to have been filled by honest toil in the study hall during the weeks before the examination. His invention was like a biggish digital watch, with two winders which operated on the principle of film spools. It was his practice to painstakingly copy out the vital information for each subject on miniature rolls of paper and insert them into the machine. It always struck me that for far less effort Billy could have learned the stuff off by heart, but that wasn't his way.

To a passing supervisor it seemed that he was simply checking the time but the year Billy did the senior certificate the supervisor was a man to whom all candidates were the enemy. He was a little bald man with thick glasses, retired from some occupation that he apparently found less than fulfilling. He formed some suspicions of Billy's constant time-checking and finally he took his answer paper away and wrote something on it.

It's a universal law that all exams are held during a heatwave, so when the supervisor arrived each morning in his pre-war Austin 7 the sliding roof was always open. That afternoon, as he was driving away from the school, past a rose-bed that was the principal's pride and job, Billy, whose aim with a handball was legendary, dropped a high one through the car's sun-roof.

The little man clutched his head with both hands and drove through the rose-bed. Game, set and match to the loser, in this case.

'Do you remember,' Billy asked me, 'the time you got expelled for breaking your man's wrist?'

'Expulsion isn't something you easily forget,' I said, 'though his wrist wasn't broken. Maybe just sprained a bit, that's all.'

It was nothing more than a minor punch-up with another pupil over some trivial matter which I have long since forgotten. He took a swipe at me which missed and he fell in a heap, which in a sense made me the winner, for at that moment a teacher was spotted coming and we scattered to the four winds.

It turned out that he was both a poor loser and a good liar. The authorities took a hand in the row – when the 'wrong' person loses they tend to – and it transpired that he was a pianist of immense potential. It was the first time anyone had ever heard this, apart from himself and the music teacher, but the music teacher's star was in the ascendant. I was ordered to be off the premises by five o'clock and never to return.

At half-past four that afternoon the order was rescinded due to the intervention of the history teacher and the English teacher, who, against all the evidence to the contrary, had apparently discerned in me the makings of a useful citizen. They were decent, scholarly men and they both said they could spot a chancer through a brick wall. One of them said he had learned a lot from being at school since he was five and the other advised me to avoid all things musical, since they didn't seem to agree with me. They were both right.

At that moment Mrs Billy popped up again. Billy turned to her.

'This is . . .' he said by way of introduction but that was as far as he got. She scanned me the way a television camera pans over a football crowd and dismissed me from her experience.

'No time now, William,' she said in the three-striped voice of authority, 'Come here, I want to show you something.'

And off they went, just like that, though my imagination suggested she was adding a word or two to Billy about talking to strangers. He looked back at me and I thought at once of the wee boy in the poem setting off for his first day at school. His feet were going forward but his head was turning back. A misspent youth is supposed to be a pleasant thing to look back on. The insights of a saint can only be gained by an apprenticeship as a sinner. I think that's what Billy's look was saying to me.

19   Breach of Promise

I did a brief spell as a barman in a local pub during the Christmas holidays of my last year in college. I wasn't exactly overworked. Rural drinking habits ran only to bottles of stout and half 'uns of whiskey, sometimes combined but mostly separately. There was no draught beer, no demand for mixers and if it wasn't stout or whiskey we hadn't got it. The clientele was exclusively male. The only women to be found in country pubs in 1959 were either the owners or the daughters of the owners.

There's no better place to stand and observe humanity than at the hatch that links the bar of a country pub with the back room. Take Dan Curran, as an example. There wasn't much I didn't find out about him during that Christmas, in one way or another.

He farmed 20 heathery acres at the foot of Mullamore and the local consensus was that he was a bit odd. He was friendly enough with me, and would occasionally recall some scrap of local history that he apparently thought might add to my store of knowledge. He mentioned my studies from time to time, being under the impression that I actually did some and that the book – a novel actually – which I kept propped up inside the hatch was a learned textbook.

Dan was normally sparing with his words but, then, he had nobody to talk to during his dawn-to-dusk existence except Annie, and you didn't talk much to Annie by all accounts. Mostly you listened. She was Dan's mother, a hardy woman in her seventies and widowed for over 40 years. She had her day of the place, as the local expression was, and that made her the boss, but then she would have been the boss anyway, no matter what the will said. The way things worked out, Dan worked the land, and the house and the yard were Annie's territory. Dan didn't interfere in Annie's domain, and in theory at least she left Dan's agricultural activities alone.

The district abounded with tales of their clashes. There was no question of Dan marrying, not while Annie was in the land of the living. The thought probably hardly crossed his mind. Annie's domestic conveyor belt provided him with clean shirts, socks and meals, which ruled out the basic need for a wife as far as a simple soul like Dan was concerned.

Annie had strong views on women, especially those younger than herself. She dismissed them as the 'ones that's going on,' in tones which suggested that they were all nothing more than painted hussies, totally unsuited to life as she understood it. Her horizons were bounded by life in the shadow of Mullamore and it would have been a tougher character than Dan who would have challenged her for a share of it.

Curiously enough, once in a while she would snap at Dan for his failure to bring in a wife to help out, but if Dan had ever made such a suggestion, it was generally agreed, she would have had a stroke.

I don't suppose Dan had give much thought to what he would have liked that Christmas, but it turned out to be a Christmas to remember, because what he got, or thought he got, was a bride. Christmas week began very wet which was why he came into the bar unusually early. The circle of damp farmers round the fire made room and I dispensed his order through the hatch.

'We were just wondering before you came in, Dan,' one of them said, 'where you'd be going on Christmas Night?' This was a reference to the local custom, then in decline, of staking a claim on a bride by visiting her house on Christmas Night, accompanied by a spokesman. Dan laughed but said nothing.

The spokesman in these cases would spend the night extolling the virtues of his client to the prospective in-laws and getting tight at the expense of the potential groom. It was all a bit of a cod, really. The girl's parents, being the suitor's neighbours, knew him and his seed, breed and generation. The matter would have been decided on long before. Even so, the Christmas Night ritual was more than a formality. It wasn't unknown for an out-and-out no-hoper to turn up, especially if the girl had well-doing parents. The old Irish proverb about marrying a woman with a laying hen was closely adhered to on Mullamore.

It was about seven o'clock that evening when Dan stepped out of the pub into the winter drizzle. I pieced together the full story of the next few days some time later.

The first hint of trouble had come when he arrived at the yard gate and met a chorus of impatient bellows from the byre. He blundered into the kitchen and found Annie lying on the sofa. Now this was something unheard of. In Annie's book, if you wanted to lie down you went to bed.

She welded him to the spot with a practised glare.

'Where were you till this time of the day? Don't tell me, you were in the pub, you idle lump, leaving me to do the milking and the feeding. Well, there'll be less of that from now on, I'm telling you.

'What happened, Ma?' he asked fearfully. 'Will I get the doctor or what?'

'I want no doctor,' snapped Annie. 'I just took a wee turn, that's all.' She rolled her eyes heavenward. 'Lord, would you look at him,' she said to the ceiling. 'Look at him, standing there with his two arms the one length. Many a one like you would have married and brought a woman in here long ago, instead of having your poor mother working her fingers to the bone. Oh, if your poor father could see you now.'

Dan was in no mood for reminiscences about his poor father. He fled to the byre where he sat on a milking stool and buried his cloth-capped head in the unaccustomed flank of a puzzled cow. As he listened to the hesitant strains of milk hitting the bottom of the bucket he contemplated his future, now that Annie had wobbled in her orbit for the first time. The future, as he saw it, was an endless vista of toil, relieved only by stewed tea and shop bread.

Then it crossed his mind that maybe there was something in Annie's latest reference to marrying. For the first time in his life he began to give serious thought to the possibility. He was so engrossed by the novelty that he barely noticed Packy, a neighbouring bachelor farmer and boozing companion, poke his head round the door. In a few terse words Dan outlined the evening's events.

'Packy,' he said, suddenly decisive, 'I'll have to marry.'

'Who will you ask?' Packy wanted to know. It wasn't an unreasonable question. Marriageable maidens were a rare species on Mullamore mountain.

'On Christmas Night,' said Dan, 'We'll go down to Cassidy's. I'll ask for Maggie and you'll put in the good word. We'll take a couple of bottles with us to help things along.'

Packy slumped down on the spare milking-stool, slack-jawed with shock. And with good reason. To be sure, Dan was no oil painting but Maggie was as near cube-shaped as it's possible for the human body to become. She was straight of hair, prominent of tooth and she looked at life through glasses that might have been hewn from the bottoms of beer bottles. With her legs permanently encased in wellingtons she didn't exactly set the pulse racing. However, she did have one very desirable attraction. As the sole offspring of her widowed and deaf-as-a-post father, she was heir to his 20 acres.

Dan kept his plans from Annie, a wise move in view of the way things worked out. On Christmas Night he and Packy made their erratic way to the Cassidy farm, well supplied with festive brew, innocent of excise duty and originating from higher up Mullamore. They had spent a good part of the afternoon sampling the stuff and when Dan told me the story later on he admitted he couldn't recall much of the night's events.

He couldn't remember arriving at Cassidy's. Or leaving it. He did have some hazy images of the massive Maggie nodding and smiling as she plied them and her father with tumblers of poteen. He also had a vague recollection of muttering at Maggie and her father. He recalled tapping each of them on the knee, and gesturing at Packy, happily snoring in the armchair by the fire. He had no notion whatsoever of what he said to either of them.

When he woke up late next morning there was a regiment of gnomes tunnelling in his skull with pneumatic drills and a smell of frying bacon drifting up from the kitchen. The realisation that he was now an engaged man catapulted him out of bed and the shock of the cold lino on his bare feet had a sobering effect as well.

He threw on his clothes and stumbled down to the kitchen where Annie was making breakfast. He viewed his indestructible mother and, in a state of near terror, imagined the awful picture of Maggie and her in the same kitchen.

'Are you alright, Ma?' he asked, tentatively.

'Certainly I'm alright,' she said and pointed to two enamel buckets of milk cooling in the pantry. 'And I'd need to be. The cows won't milk themselves, you know. Lord knows what would happen to them if they were left to the likes of you.'

Dan grabbed his coat and cap from behind the door and retreated to the yard where he leaned on the gable wall of the barn and looked down towards Cassidy's farm. The wind coming off the top of Mullamore was like a knife around his ears. Then Annie came to the door and spoke to her only son in sawmill tones.

'Do you know how you got home this morning?' she demanded. And she went on to tell him. He didn't believe it at first but there had been other revellers around and half the parish could confirm, before Boxing Day was over, that he had made transport history by being brought home in a wheelbarrow. There was also general agreement that Maggie Cassidy had the makings of a great navvy and that Packy couldn't sing a note.

'Come on in and take your breakfast,' Annie said maliciously. 'What you need now is a big plate of bacon and eggs and fried bread.'

Dan needed nothing of the sort. He crammed his cap against his mouth and fled round the end of the barn to be sick. By the time he had recovered he knew there was only one course open to him. He straightened his shoulders and set off for the Cassidy farm. Cassidy was walking across the yard when he arrived.

'A hardy morning that, Dan,' he said. 'How's the form after last night?'

Dan cannily kept the gate between them and got straight to the point.

'I just came down to tell you,' he said gruffly, 'that Ma's all right again, so I won't be needing Maggie after all.'

Cassidy leaned on the gate and Dan braced himself for the storm.

'It's a funny thing, Dan, but I never knew Packy had a notion of Maggie,' he said. 'Now, no harm to you, Dan, but he didn't need you or anybody to put in a word for him. He's a decent, hardworking man and a great match for Maggie. He just walked up here the night before Christmas Eve and asked her, straight out, here at this gate. It's not the old way, Dan, but sure we have to move with the times.'

Dan stood shaking with mixed emotions at this revelation. Of course he was relieved that Cassidy had missed the point of the whole thing from the start. At the same time, he was annoyed at the wily Packy getting in ahead or him, even if the price for an extra 20 acres was more than Dan was willing to pay.

It all made sense, Packy's surprise at Dan's sudden decision to marry, Packy getting him tight on Christmas Day on the near-lethal rot-gut from the mountain. He heard Cassidy's voice, as from a distance.

'You're not looking at all well, Dan,' he said. 'Come on in for a hair of the dog.'

'I won't bother,' said Dan. 'I'm going to give it up. It causes nothing but trouble.'

'Ah, come on in anyway,' Cassidy rumbled on. 'Have something to eat. Maggie's frying bacon and eggs.'

'Aw, Gawd, not more bacon,' moaned Dan and he crammed the cap against his face and set off for home at a half-gallop.

The next afternoon he was cycling past the pub whistling, as I was opening the door.

'What did you get for Christmas, Dan?' I called out.

'A reprieve,' he shouted back.

That, indeed, is what he got, but the ancient Christmas Night custom was gone forever.

20 Home Again to Wales

The summer of 1959 saw me back in Wales, this time in the south of the Principality. Wimpeys were laying an oil pipeline across an 18-mile stretch of countryside as part of a vast oil terminal complex and Charlie O'Kane had written to offer me a job on the project. I was to be part of a back-filling squad. Our task was to restore the countryside to its original state after the contractor's machines and work-force had passed through.

In the event I never functioned as one of those pick-and-shovel conservationists. I had been told to be in Carmarthen by three o'clock on the appointed afternoon. There I would meet the rest of the group and we would all travel by lorry to begin our labours in the region of Pontardulais. I didn't reach Carmarthen until after six and there wasn't a Wimpey's vehicle in sight. There was no reply when I called the transport yard at Pontardulais. A careful dredging through my pockets rounded up just over a pound in small change. It was going to be a long, hungry night.

I spent it in what was described as a bed-and-breakfast place. My cash supply, I found out, ran only to a bed and I couldn't have that until 11 o'clock either. When the landlord eventually showed me to it, the previous occupant was still in the act of getting out of it. The bed worked shifts, I discovered. Every eight hours a new body occupied it and neither time nor money were wasted in fripperies like changing the sheets. Still, beggars – or homeless navvies with only a pound to their names – can't be choosers. I slept soundly and hit the street soon after seven, a pound poorer but happy to discover that not a single, microscopic life form had attached itself to my person during the night.

My next call to the transport yard was answered with raging apathy until I mentioned Charlie O'Kane's name, whereupon I was told to stay exactly where I was and a lorry would pick me up immediately. Four hours later the vehicle arrived. I hardly heard it draw up, for the sound of the engine was practically drowned out by the thunderous protests from my stomach. The driver informed me that all the back-filling squads were at full strength as from three o'clock on the previous day. It seemed I was on the way to Pontardulais to become unemployed. I had some doubts about even getting there when he explained that he was late because he had to make a detour to pick up some dynamite. The stuff was slewing around in the back and I kept a watchful eye on it in the rear-view mirror all the way to Pontardulais.

Good news awaited me on arrival. By a stroke of the administrative pen I had been transformed in absentia from back-filler to welder's mate and I was given an advance of nine pounds. For a hungry man, what better bonus could there be than finding that the digs which had been arranged for him were in the local butcher's. I was reminded to be at the yard no later than a quarter-to-seven in the morning to meet a van that would deliver me to the line. There was organisation behind the apparent chaos.

The butcher's shop occupied part of the ground floor of a large house and the owner and his wife supplemented their income by keeping construction workers. They were great digs. There can't have been many others where, last thing before bedtime, the landlady placed a huge dish of fried sausages in the middle of the table and ordered the lodgers to consume the lot.

The welders were the aristocrats of the site and the duties of a welder's mate were numerous but not too demanding. As far as the company was concerned, a welder's mate existed to ensure that the joints of the 18-inch pipes were ready for X-ray. The pipes were welded in long sections mounted on trestles beside the trench and the welding process left behind a metallic crust that had to be laborously removed using a pad saw and a wire brush. The faintest speck of crust showed up on the final X-ray, which meant that the joint had to be broken and welded again.

The welders were all on bonus. The wrath of a welder whose joint failed the test was terrible to behold. When you take into account that they were, to the last man, ex-Clydeside shipyard workers, fellows who had elevated swearing to an art form, it can be seen that it was unwise to put their financial situation at risk. I was lucky. None of the joints I cleaned failed the X-ray.

I did fall short of expectations in other ways. There was, for example, the incident of the snake. Power for the welding equipment was produced by mobile generators, and it was part of my job to stow the heavy-duty cables in the storage compartment on top of the engine every day when we finished work. I also had to connect them up again in the morning.

One morning I reached into the storage compartment and found that instead of an inert and shiny cable I was holding something warm and scaly. The compressor had been parked in the corner of a field overnight but at the time I attached no significance to that. I hauled the object out and found that I was holding a snake by the scruff of what would have been its neck, if it had had a neck. It eyed me with its beady eyes and flickered its forked tongue. I stared back, with open mouth. This stalemate lasted for perhaps a hundredth of a second.

'Snake!' I yelled at the top of my voice and dropped the reptile back into the storage compartment.

Panic spread among the ranks of the sluggish, early morning work-force. 'Snake!' they shouted, and scattered in all directions. As I led the stampede out of the field I found my two welders seated on a rock reading the racing pages.

'You,' said one of them, 'go down to the wee pub and get me a couple of bottles of light ale.'

This kind of menial activity was part of a welder's mate's duties. It had numerous pitfalls, not the least of them being the difficulty of getting money from the welders. Like royalty, these lordly creatures didn't seem to carry cash.

'It's only seven o'clock in the morning,' I told him.

'Listen,' said the welder,' If I want to know the time I'll look at my watch.'

'Where's everybody going?' demanded the second welder.

'There's a snake in the compressor,' I said.

'Well, get rid of it,' snarled the second welder. 'I can't make any money sitting here.'

'Are you going for the beer or not?' the first welder asked crossly.

'No,' I said, firmly. I didn't relish waking up a country publican in the middle of Wales on such an errand. That sort of thing is fine for Ireland, but the Welsh have a healthier regard for the law and tend to observe it even when they aren't being watched.

'Bloody firm's man,' growled the welder and went back to the racing page.

Geordie, the foreman, drew up in his yellow landrover.

'What's going on here?' he demanded. The welders ignored him.

'Well, you tell me,' he said to me. 'Why hasn't work started?'

He was on bonus, too, and reputed to be the highest earner on the line.

'There's a snake in the compressor,' I said.

'You're responsible for the compressor,' said Geordie. 'Get rid of the bloody snake. That's your job.'

The fleeing work-force had shuffled back by this time and were taking a close interest in the proceedings.

'There are no snakes in Wales,' the first welder looked up from his racing page. 'He just made that story up. He doesn't want to go down and get me a couple of bottles of light ale from that pub. He's just a bloody firm's man.'

Billy Watkins, barrack-room lawyer and travelling encyclopedia of union rules and safety regulations, spoke up.

'This man can't touch the snake,' he declared. 'He's a student. If he gets bitten and dies, there'll be trouble with the head of his college.'

I didn't think, somehow, that the head of my college would have created much of a disturbance, for two good reasons. One was that I had completed my exams at the start of that summer and the other was that I had preferred to take the remunerative Welsh job than to dress up to attend my own graduation.

An hour passed. The sun rose higher and so did the cigarette smoke. The welders reconciled themselves to lost bonus and composed themselves to sleep on the rock. Then a company official arrived. He was known officially as the expediter and he enquired in a loud voice why all these illegitimate persons were lying around at such enormous expense to the company.

Geordie explained about the snake in the compressor. The expediter looked disbelieving. I added my personal authority to the matter. The expediter swore volubly. At the tail-end of this discussion, a local farm labourer rode up on his bike. He propped the bike against the gatepost and sauntered down the field towards the compressor. We tagged along behind at a safe distance. He lifted the top of the storage box and in the most unconcerned manner possible lifted out the snake. It was about four feet long and wriggling crossly.

'Grass snake,' said the Welshman laconically. 'Completely harmless.' He threw it casually over the hedge into the next field. 'There's a lot of them in these parts.' he added and passed through our midst on the way to his bike with a smirk on his face. We all went sheepishly back to work.

The welders brought nothing but themselves to work. At lunch-time they plundered freely from any neighbouring lunch-box or flask, so it was important to bring extra sandwiches or risk starvation. They were sore on sunglasses, too, but never bought any, so I found it necessary keep a couple of cheap pairs in reserve. The sunglasses were no idle luxury. When a welding rod made contact with a section of pipe it gave off a blinding flash which dried the moisture from unprotected eyeballs and eyelids. The result was extremely uncomfortable. The eyes felt as though they had been instantly lined with coarse sandpaper. They streamed constantly, as in a bout of hay fever, and the only relief was to lie down in a darkened room for about 12 hours, though sleep was impossible.

In spite of their protective helmets, the welders wore sun-glasses as an extra precaution. To be precise, they wore mine. The supply of food, drink and sunglasses, apart from cleaning the joints and running their messages, was all part of the rich experience of being a welder's mate.

There were other experiences that made a lasting impression on me. For example, there was the August Bank Holiday of that year, made eternally memorable for me because I lost a bulldozer. It's not easy to lose a bulldozer but with practice, persistence and the right amount of misfortune, you can occasionally achieve remarkable things.

Work came to a standstill on the Friday and the work-force scattered in all directions, except for me. I had nowhere to go, a fact that Charlie O'Kane had duly noted. He turned up at lunch-time that day with a proposition. If I was willing to act as a temporary security officer over the weekend, he, for his part, would ensure that the company rewarded me at treble the usual rate. He gave me a list of the company's earthmoving equipment and the precise location of each machine along the cross-country line. My job was to take a bus out to the farthest end of the line and walk back across several miles of farmland, wade across several streams and tick off each item as I passed it. The return trip ended just outside Pontardulais and I had only to carry these onerous tasks out twice daily, once in the morning and again in the afternoon. Money for old rope, really.

I had another security responsibility that weekend. My landlord and landlady had a teenage son at that awkward age, too old to go with them to Devon for the holiday, too young to be left unsupervised. His mother felt that since I was considered responsible enough to be left in charge of millions of pounds worth of machinery I could easily keep an eye on young Robert as well.

Robert's unwillingness to go to Devon had nothing to do with being too old to go and everything to do with Myfanwy, his girlfriend. I can never hear the Treorchy Male Choir in full voice praising their Myfanwy without associating the name with a missing bulldozer and a dead budgie, of which more anon. I entered into an immediate pact with Robert. If he was in the house when I was there, that was one thing. I couldn't be responsible for where he was, or what he was doing, when I was walking the line. This was the somewhat lyrical name for my security job. When I left the house on Saturday morning for my first patrol Robert was consuming tea and toast in the kitchen in a virtuous manner. Some time was to pass before I saw him again.

Every dumper, crane, sideboom, tractor and bulldozer was exactly where it had been left. It was a blazing hot day and my progress was leisurely, in fact it was mid-afternoon before I arrived back in Pontardulais. Halfway down the street I met a Welsh workmate with the improbable name of Doug O'Reilly. He was accompanied by sundry other happy souls, all of them on the way to a wedding reception in the hotel.

'Come with us,' said Doug. 'Nobody will mind. Friend of ours and all that.'

'But I have to check on the machines,' I protested, half-heartedly. Forget the machines was Doug's cheerful advice.

'They'll be all right. Nobody's going to steal 'em, see.' So I forgot the machines, nipped smartly into the digs and did a quick-change routine while Doug and company sang a few soulful verses in the otherwise deserted street. There was no sign of Robert.

The afternoon patrol was carried out from the comfort of the hotel lounge. In fact, between the wedding and my own inability to get my back off the mattress the next morning, it was well into Sunday afternoon before I checked my charges. Robert was safely at home and each machine was in its ordained place. Until I reached the very end of the line.

It was marked by a temporary wire fence to replace the hedge that had previously bounded the road. According to my list, and the evidence of my last visit, many thousand pounds worth of bulldozer should have been parked there, with its gleaming blade nuzzling cosily up against the fence. There was no bulldozer. No tell-tale caterpillar tracks marked the ground around the parking spot, but heavy duty tyres had left their imprint on the grass verge outside. The bulldozer had been spirited away on a low-loader.

I sat down for a while and considered my suddenly bleak future. Assuming my current rate of pay, and even living on air, it would take a minimum of 10 years to repay the company for the loss of the machine. Whatever move I made would make things worse. I could hardly go to the police, for it was bound to come out that I had missed two patrols. There was every chance that some law-abiding person had witnessed the theft of the bulldozer – it's a difficult thing to steal secretly – and timed it during the time I was hooleying at the wedding feast. There was also the effect on Charlie O'Kane's career to be considered. His judgement was likely to be forever suspect, once it came out that he had left the company's machines in the charge of a man who couldn't even be relied on to go out and count them twice a day.

Since I was the company's sole representative in the area that weekend, there was no one I could report to. It was a gloomy security man who jolted homewards on the bus that afternoon. When I got in I was only mildly surprised to find that Robert was missing, too. I was just beginning to form an idea of how Job felt when a thunderous knocking threatened to take the shop door off its hinges. I crept up to the front bedroom window but I couldn't see the cause of the ructions. There was no police car outside, which was some sort of relief. The hammering continued.

I thought that if I kept quiet the racket would stop, but all that happened was that doors opened across the street and people peered out to see what the row was about. I gave in and opened the hall door. Outside stood an Irishman about the size of County

Tyrone, roaring drunk and demanding beef. He was a ganger on the pipeline and he was well known all the way to Milford Haven for several reasons.

The love of his life, apart from drink, was his car, which he polished and shone on the outside, and scrubbed and shampooed inside, at every possible opportunity. He was nick-named the Missing Link. He went on frequent benders that lasted anything from a couple of days to a week and his first action as soon as he turned up on site after one of these absences was to sack everyone in sight. He had reached new heights the previous week when he invaded a hut near the pipeline and sacked all eight occupants. They found it amusing and went on playing cards. Rightly so, too, for they were miners on their lunch-break, with no more connection with George Wimpey and Company than the man in the moon. There was a fellow on the site madly in love with him. This character, a disbarred barrister, followed him around like a pup, so closely at times that he actually trod on his heels. The ganger was the only man on the line who was unaware of this adulation, and nobody was foolhardy enough to tell him.

On this particular Sunday, I informed him that the butcher was in Devon, the shop was locked and that I knew nothing whatever about the meat trade. He, in turn, told me that he would come in and help himself. At this point I became, by default, something of a folk hero, though some time was to pass before my fame was noised abroad. There I was, a man who had just lost many thousand pounds worth of bulldozer, and the son of the house, value unspecified but likely to be even greater, faced with yet another disaster, the invasion of his landlord's butcher shop. Something, as they say, snapped. The irresistible force was on a collision course with the immoveable object, though at that precise moment it would have been difficult to say which was which.

I told the Missing Link that under no circumstances imaginable would he enter the premises. He laughed at this and made to sweep me aside, a move that would normally have merged me with the wallpaper. At that moment the tide in my affairs, as well as the worm, turned. My eye fell on an iron bar, three feet long and an inch-and-a-half thick, belonging to the butcher's fridge but for some inexplicable reason, just then standing inside the door. I picked it up and offered to bend it over his head. Something of my desperate urge to get one lousy thing right that weekend must have communicated itself to him. He backed out and walked away, meatless, in the direction of his flat at the end of the street.

I began to feel that things were on the turn from that point. Robert, it's true, didn't come home that night. I would have heard him, for I didn't close an eye, though I should say that my concern was for the bulldozer and the decent man from Kilrea, rather than Robert's morals.

The next morning I was the only passenger on the first bus out of the village and I covered that line in a blur of arms and legs. Every machine stood where I had last seen it and as I forded the last stream my heart soared like a lark. The marvellous, wonderful, missing bulldozer stood with its blade nestling against the fence and there was a heavy smell of warm oil in the air, the headiest perfume I had ever experienced.

When I rambled happily back into the digs the landlady, back early from Devon, was energetically cuffing Robert's ears. His secret wasn't out, because he had apparently got back after I left before she arrived. But he had, she claimed, left the back door open and the cat had got in and eaten the budgie. Maybe he did leave it open as he sneaked in, or maybe I did as I went out, for I had weightier matters on my mind.

I was never able to shake off the lingering suspicion that Doug had stage-managed my wedding invitation, so that one of his friends could do a homer with the bulldozer. He was an elusive character, whose driving duties took him all over the project. I had my mind made up to tackle him on the subject before I left the job but it wasn't to be. A couple of weeks after the bulldozer was returned, two letters arrived together at the digs. One was from the Inland Revenue in Swansea, but it was a clerical error, for I was officially still a student and exempt from income tax but I kept it as a souvenir. It's the only official communication I have ever received in Welsh.

The other letter was from Malachy, informing me that I was a hot contender for a teaching job in a country school near Drapers-town and advising me to hasten home to stake my claim to it. I turned in my company wellies and waterproof gear at the stores and, with mixed feelings, took the train for Liverpool and home.

They were even more mixed when the following Christmas the company sent me my holiday pay. I'd only been with them for two months but the holiday pay was more than my first month's pay cheque from the Ministry of Education. And the crack was better with the company, too.

ST. MARY'S COLLEGE
TRENCH HOUSE
BELFAST BT11 9GA

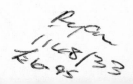